Personality, Learning and Teaching

STUDENTS LIBRARY OF EDUCATION

Personality, Learning and Teaching

George D. Handley
Senior Lecturer in Education
Kingston-upon-Hull College of Education

ROUTLEDGE & KEGAN PAUL
LONDON AND BOSTON

First published in 1973
by Routledge & Kegan Paul Ltd
Broadway House, 68-74 Carter Lane,
London EC4V 5EL and
9 Park Street,
Boston, Mass. 02108, U.S.A.
Printed in Great Britain by
Northumberland Press Limited
Gateshead
ISBN 0 7100 7625 8 (c)
0 7100 7628 2 (p)
Library of Congress Catalog Card Number 73-77564

The Students Library of Education has been designed to meet the needs of students of Education at Colleges of Education and at University Institutes and Departments. It will also be valuable for practising teachers and educationists. The series takes full account of the latest developments in teacher-training, and of new methods and approaches in education. Separate volumes will provide authoritative and up-to-date accounts of the topics within the major fields of sociology, philosophy and history of education, educational psychology, and method. Care has been taken that specialist topics are treated lucidly and usefully for the non-specialist reader. Altogether, the Students Library of Education will provide a comprehensive introduction and guide to anyone concerned with the study of education, and with educational theory and practice.

One of the curious paradoxes about education in the first half of the twentieth century, particularly in England, was that an increasing emphasis on the development of the whole child, on children and teachers as persons, and on the central role of relationships, was accompanied by an increasing tendency in academic psychology to atomize and de-humanize the person into an aggregate of behavioural units, each apparently capable of being 'fully explained' within a system of mechanistic concepts ultimately derived from (an old-fashioned) physics. In recent years this trend in psychological thinking has begun to be reversed and the characteristics of man as a personal being, as well as a machine and an organism, are beginning to be re-emphasized.

If enlightened educational thought and psychological theory are to be more compatible in the second half of the century, as it is obviously desirable they should be, this will depend to some extent on a re-evaluation of the work of the modern pioneers in the study of personality, some appreciation by students and teachers of how their own views have been, or have failed to be, influenced by the major insights of the recent past. To introduce students to this complex and developing field is a formidable task. Mr Handley's book is a vigorous and courageous attempt to do this. From the wide range of concepts of personality which exist he has chosen to describe the work of four influential psychologists, Freud, Adler, Eysenck and Allport, partly for the intrinsic interest of each and partly from the illuminating contrasts which they provide.

This is an area of study in which both sympathetic understanding and critical thought are called for from the student. Mr Handley himself sets an example. Not all will agree with his opinions and conclusions, and this is as it should be. The test is whether the discussion of different theories, their strengths and weaknesses, can illumine both learning and teaching, that is, can inform the practice of education. This is where Mr Handley himself places the emphasis and his book is to be seen as a contribution to this process.

BEN MORRIS

Contents

CONTENTS

Preface and acknowledgments

Whilst on the staff of Westminster College of Education, I became intrigued by the problems of why some practising students taught well and others badly. My long-standing interest in the psychology of personality led me to look at this question, and this book grew out of courses in personality as it relates to learning and teaching.

Acknowledgments are due to Gordon Dennis, Steve Phillipson and Donald Smith who spurred my thinking or who read and commented on parts of the book. Thanks also to my wife, Rosemary, who has always shown a keen interest in my project. In particular, I wish to thank Elisabeth Heckmann who read the whole manuscript. Her comment that the book gives the impression that the basic requirements of a good teacher are practically unattainable leads me to say to the student-teachers who may read it that one *can* be an effective teacher even if one possesses only a fraction of the basic desirable qualities. The struggle for the ideal should never dismay the existent good, rather spur it on to greater things, but the vision of the ideal does need to be with us. Browning summed up the situation:

> ... a man's reach should exceed his grasp,
> Or what's a heaven for?

1

The need for personality study

The twentieth-century world presents the individual with a much wider field of choice of career than faced him in past centuries. There are now some fifty thousand different occupations to choose from, and only rarely is the young person predestined by his parents for a particular career. Gone are the simpler days of Miss Austen when the eldest son, regardless of inclination, became a soldier and the youngest a minister of religion. One might almost wonder which is the less desirable alternative: to be forced into a job for which one is temperamentally unsuited or to be confronted with a vast number of possibilities none of which stands out from the others as being the obvious correct choice. The social and economic organization of modern society is exceedingly complex and this imposes considerable strain on its members. Width of scope brings with it a greater burden of choice and the anxiety associated with making the right decision. Because there are so many jobs to choose from, how can one know which to choose? It is said that one can never know another person except by living with him: similarly, is there any way of knowing a job except by doing it? Must first-hand experience decide the issue? Not infrequently it has to, and this, coupled with the comparative ease of mobility from one job to another, accounts for the number of changes of occupation that seem to occur in the late twenties and early thirties. Part of the restlessness of society derives from the lack of vocational guidance in schools, and possibly as the latter increases the restlessness will diminish.

More than thirty years' research into delinquency in America has made it possible for Sheldon and Eleanor Glueck (1959) to predict delinquency by considering factors in the family environment. They envisage the day when sentencing in the courts will be individualized, so that when a boy's background and personality are taken into account his particular sentence will be of a kind known from experience to work with other boys from similar backgrounds and with similar personalities. If in the past probation has been found to work with certain types of boy though not with others, this is a guide to sentencing in future. No method of dealing with the delinquent—probation, detention centres, fines, corrective training, remand homes—works with every case, but each method is effective with some. To match the particular sentence with the personality and background experience of the offender seems an eminently sensible idea, and makes the judge's role, according to the Gluecks, approach that of the social physician envisaged by Aristotle. If likelihood of success can be predicted in treating delinquents, why can it not be predicted in selecting would-be teachers? It would be most useful if some testing instrument could be devised which would enable us to know before a student embarks on a teacher training course whether his personality and background make him likely to succeed in the profession. The thinking that would need to precede the construction of such a test is very considerable: some of the problems involved in the analysis of the criterion are discussed in chapter 7.

Attempts to determine the criteria for success in teaching have been made, and it is one of the purposes of this book to look at some of these. Assessments, such as those made by colleges of education, are bound to contain some degree of subjectivity, and the evidence comparing college teaching marks with later ratings suggests that the college mark is not as good a guide to future teaching performance as one might hope. However, even the best of teachers will admit that there are some classes with which he or she feels less successful than with others. This may be quite independent of the pupils' ages or abilities. It poses another problem and brings us to the second part of our quest: why is it that one teacher succeeds with certain pupils but not with others? Again, why is it that two boys, with roughly equivalent I.Q. scores, ages and socio-economic backgrounds, are so different in their attainments? Why does one do better in all subjects than the other? Will it always be the same one who is the more successful? The recent upsurge of interest in creativity has indicated that, particularly as regards the field in which a pupil is successful, personality factors are important. It seems probable that if a person has the minimum of intelligence required for success in a particular field, then whether he performs well or badly in that field will be crucially affected by non-intellective factors. Hudson (1966) claims rightly that the academically successful boy is distinguished by the use he sees fit to make of his intellectual apparatus rather than simply by its possession.

Psychology, in trying to be scientific, is bound to deal in generalized statements and these have severe limitations which will become more apparent in chapter 5, where the viewpoints of Allport and Eysenck are discussed. For the present it will be useful to bear in mind some words of John Macmurray (1935): 'Science is concerned with generalities, with more or less universal characteristics of things in general, not with anything in particular. And anything real is always something in particular.' Teachers must remember that psychological statements about children should not be expected to fit every child. Individual differences must always be taken into account.

The psychology of learning, itself a vast study, is by no means the only field of psychology which is of value to the teacher. Explorations in personality and human relationships are equally important though they seem to have received comparatively little attention in most British textbooks of educational psychology. Understanding his cognitive processes is far from understanding the child, and the process of education involves his personality as a whole. Morris (1966), discussing the relevance of psychological thought to educational thought, reminds us that psychology has relevance to education only when man is considered as a *person* rather than according to an organismic or a mechanistic model. Even as long ago as the fourteenth century, Chaucer (Coghill, 1951) recognized the importance of happiness as the prerequisite of successful learning: 'The happy child will always learn and hear'—and twentieth-century psychiatrists recognize prolonged unhappiness as a key symptom of the maladjusted personality which is linked with failure to make progress in school. The study of personality helps one to understand other people, and the teacher needs to understand his pupils.

He also needs to understand himself. The teacher who has explored his own personality, who has insight into himself, will be better equipped to train others in understanding themselves, their strengths and limitations. To know oneself superficially is not enough; this leaves one blind to one's own irrationalities, and makes maturity an impossibility. The experience of sharing the insights of psychology into the nature of personality is highly beneficial (Morris, 1972).

Largely because of its eagerness for scientific status,

4

psychology, up to about 1960, had tended to become dehumanized; the person had been reified, made into a thing, nothing more than an aggregate of stimuli and responses. To do this is to make the *person* unreal. By the mid-sixties, however, there was evidence that psychology was 'regaining Consciousness' (see Joynson, 1972). Some writers recognized the value and importance of subjective experience as well as of objective behaviour (see, for example, McKellar, 1968) though comprehensive behaviouristic explanations of man are still being offered (e.g. Skinner, 1971). Man cannot be reduced to a formula, nor can his psychic parts be studied in isolation from one another. Of man it may be truly said that the whole is more than the sum of the parts, much more.

The teaching process and the learning process cannot be looked at in isolation from personality. Neither can the personality of the teacher and that of the learner be looked at in isolation from each other. Human interaction is a field of study currently being explored and some reference to this must be made in the final chapter.

The aim of this book is to show the importance of non-intellective factors in the processes of teaching and learning by a consideration of the psychology of personality. The following chapter attempts to define personality and to relate it to theory. Then we examine, in chapters 3, 4 and 5, the insights of a small selection of personality theorists, and the final chapters blend empirical study and speculation in considering aspects of personality in relation to teaching and learning success.

2

Personality and theory

Personality

Psychology clearly has a contribution to make to the theory and practice of education. It is therefore included in courses for those who train to teach. This part of the course is generally called the psychology of education and it pays particular attention to the study of the learning process. Such a bias seems reasonable because learning is at the heart of education. But educational psychology can become too narrow unless, whilst emphasizing learning, it takes into account other processes. Although some learning occurs incidentally and some occurs because it is immediately related to the subject's needs, much of the learning that goes on in school depends on the teacher's arousing of motivation. The whole process of motivation has central relevance in education; this process in relation with learning needs consideration. Likewise the effects of emotion on learning, of perception, and so on. All aspects of human functioning interact, and learning cannot be considered in isolation from the other aspects.

Motivation is a central concept in the psychology of personality. This field is much wider than the psychology of learning: it is concerned with the functioning of the total

6

individual. The student of personality will be glad to use the findings of those who have directed their research to specific aspects of mental functioning such as learning or memory or perception, but such segmental study of behaviour represents only a number of parts. The student of personality is interested in restructuring or integrating the parts so as to understand the individual as a whole. He may be thought of, rather romantically, as the one who puts together the parts of a jigsaw puzzle. He will obtain the parts from various investigators: the experimental psychologist, the clinical psychologist, the human biologist, the sociologist and the anthropologist, to mention only some. The theorists of personality considered in the middle section of this book have used different kinds of part in differing degrees.

The final description and explanation of personality given by any theorist will depend therefore on his particular preference for one field of investigation rather than another. This is why a definition of personality which is totally free from bias is so hard to give. Any particular theorist will describe personality in terms of those explanatory concepts which to him seem most significant. His definition of personality will reflect this. If, for example, he considers that personality is formed largely as a result of our falling in with what we believe others expect of us, his definition will be very different from that given by one who emphasizes the biological or institutional determinants of personality. Any definition depends on the theoretical framework out of which it grows.

Though a preferred definition of personality will not be given in this book, a few examples may be found helpful. Personality may be viewed in terms of its external effect: thus it is claimed to be the sum total of the effect made by an individual on society. If this definition seems to be too much concerned with what man *seems* to be and to neglect his essential nature, we may prefer to call personality the sum total of ways in which one individual differs from another. Akin to this, but rather more epigrammatic, is Notcutt's definition of personality as the pattern of an individual life (Notcutt, 1953). Some would argue that if this is what personality is, it is no concern of scientific psychologists; for them personality would be that which makes us able to predict how a person will behave in given situations.

Though an unequivocal definition of what personality is will not be offered, a word must be said about what, for the psychologist, personality is not. It is not something which Susan has but Mary has not; this is implied by the common phrase, 'a girl with personality' or the statement, 'She has no personality'. These are psychologically nonsensical: the first is tautologous (being a girl *means* having personality), the second, a contradiction in terms. From the standpoint of psychology, personality is a necessary attribute of being a person—one's personality is that particular cluster of characteristics making one different from all others. Courses in cultivating personality are not aimed at producing personality where formerly there was none but at creating a certain type of personality valued by a section of society.

Personality is not a value-word. Properly speaking, it does not refer to something which it is desirable to have. In common usage the term is often confused with character. At its simplest, personality is concerned with how things are; character with how things ought or ought not to be. Character implies a moral standard. It refers to that pattern of characteristics which happen to be morally approved or disapproved in a society. It may usefully be thought of as personality evaluated (Allport, 1963). The distinction is worth remembering.

8

Theory

Theory is a word which is often used antithetically in relation to practice. Thus one who is training to teach is taught both the theory and practice of education. The latter usually consists of time spent in schools and is generally (and probably rightly) believed to be the most valuable part of the training. The former consists of a set of ideas—one hopes of explicitly inter-related ideas—brought together from various disciplines and relevant to the subject of teaching. Strictly there cannot be said to be a theory unless the ideas expressed are systematically inter-related, though the term is often loosely used to refer to any piece of speculation.

Hall and Lindzey (1957) define a theory as a set of conventions which are chosen in a quite arbitrary way and put together creatively by the theorist. He is entitled to choose whatever ideas he wishes for inclusion in his theory; this is a creative act akin to that of a novelist or a poet. It differs only in the kinds of evidence mainly used and in the crittria which will be used in its evaluation. No one can give rules or formulae for constructing theories—here the theorist, like the poet or novelist, is free; but there are specifications as to how a theory should be judged and evaluated.

Hall and Lindzey also hold that a theory is never true or false. These adjectives may be applied only to the implications of or derivations from a theory. The theory itself is not determined by known facts, that is, by proven connections with observable phenomena; it goes beyond these and cannot therefore be described as true or false. However, a theory may be described as useful or not useful depending how far it generates relevant ideas which stand the test of empirical verification and therefore add to what is already known.

Though we cannot provide a formula for theory construction, there are certain criteria which a theory, to be acceptable as such, should fulfil, just as there are certain criteria which a piece of writing must fulfil to be acceptable as a poem. First, the assumptions included in a theory must be relevant: they must bear upon the subject-matter of the theory. Thus a theory of personality must be made up of statements about personality. Where statements are made about the elements of personality, the relation of the elements to the whole should be clear. Second, the assumptions made should be systematically related to one another. It must be clear how A is linked with B: contradictions, *non sequiturs* and other illogicalities must be excluded. Just as good language usage involves the conventions of grammar or syntax, so a good theory is logically consistent. It conforms to the syntax of theory. Third, for a theory, at least in science, to be evaluated, it must be capable of what Hall and Lindzey call *empirical translation*, that is to say, it must be possible to discover objects or events in the real world to which the concepts used in the theory correspond. To satisfy the scientist and the logical positivist, these objects or events must be publicly observable, publicly available to sense experience, not purely subjective and observable only to the proponent of the theory in some internal way. Unless the concepts used in the theory can be translated in this way, the only test of the theory is its internal consistency, and, because it cannot be empirically verified, it can never add to the sum total of what is known.

This brings us to the question of what a theory is supposed to do: what are its functions? There are two main ones: (1) a theory should be an attempt to organize and integrate what is known. This is something which is plainly valuable. Thus a theory of learning should embrace all the dependable information about the learning process available at the time when the theory is constructed; furthermore it should do this in such a way that inconsistent findings are reconciled as far as possible. Of course the theorist's view of what is dependable information may not be based on the rather narrow criterion of the logical positivists mentioned above: what constitutes adequate evidence is still an unresolved question. However, any theory should begin from this point—the organizing of the relevant facts. This may be called the *inductive* phase. (2) The theory should then proceed to what might be called a *predictive* phase. Here the theorist brings his mind to bear on the dependable information in such a way as to indicate new relations between what is known and, implicitly or explicitly, to suggest strategies for future research. On the basis of the information, hypotheses are inferred, generalizations and predictions made. The extent to which this part of a theory serves as a spur to research by suggesting appropriate ideas, or even the extent to which it provokes disbelief or resistance, may be called its heuristic influence, and Hall and Lindzey consider this the most valuable indication of a theory's effectiveness.

We have now considered what theories are designed to do and are in a better position to judge how well the small sample of theories in this book fulfil their function. In fact, no theory of personality so far developed adequately fulfils the criteria for a good theory. Each falls down in some respect, but this does not mean attempts to formulate such a theory should stop. Assumptions about personality are implicit in all attempts to interpret human behaviour and it seems right that someone should attempt to systematize these and make them explicit. Furthermore, once a theory has been drawn up, it does, as we have seen, serve to clarify research objectives and, as Hebb (1951) contends, the rubble of bad theories is a prerequisite for the building of better ones. All existing theories will undoubtedly contribute something to the ultimate understanding of man's personality and this will make for an increase in the quality and effectiveness of living in all its aspects, not least the educational ones which are our present concern.

3

The Freudian account of personality

Sigmund Freud (1856-1939)

Sigmund Freud called himself a 'godless Jew'. He was proud
to be a Jew, but his attitude to religion, even the Jewish
religion, was critically negative. Throughout his long life,
he appears to have felt no need to believe in God and seems
to have regarded religion as an illusion, a universal neurosis
and a support for the emotionally inadequate. His sensitivity to anti-Semitic feeling reached a climax when in
1938 Hitler's invasion of Austria obliged him to leave
Vienna, where he had lived for nearly eighty years, to
end his days in London.

He was born in Freiburg, Moravia, in May 1856, the
eldest child of his mother and the third son of his father,
Jakob. It must have seemed curious to the young Sigmund
to discover that his playmate, John, who was slightly older
and stronger than he, was in fact his nephew. John was
the son of Sigmund's half-brother, born of his father's first
wife. Sigmund regarded his mother as being the wife of
his other adult half-brother, Philipp, his father being paired
in the toddler's mind with his nannie. Being born an uncle
was but one of the many paradoxical family relationships
his young mind had to grapple with, and, as his biographer,

Ernest Jones (1953), suggests, it doubtless served as an incentive to his growing intelligence.

Jakob Freud was a wool merchant, and when Sigmund was three, because of financial difficulties, the family had to leave Freiburg. After a year in Leipzig, they settled in Vienna, though by this time the family situation was less complicated, the two elder half-brothers having gone to England, the nannie being dismissed. Jakob recognized his son's intellectual potential—he once laughingly claimed that his son's little toe was cleverer than his own head—and, though poor, made sure Sigmund had a good education. The boy was his mother's favourite and this gave him confidence in himself which, coupled with his ability and industry, inevitably led to success.

He enrolled as a medical student in the University of Vienna at seventeen, and in 1881 he qualified and began working in the Vienna General Hospital. He was particularly interested in neuro-anatomy and neuropathology, and, because of his interest in nervous disorders, worked hard for the opportunity to go to Paris to see the work of Dr Charcot, who was using hypnosis to cure hysterical patients in an asylum there. When he returned to Vienna in 1886 Freud established himself in private practice to treat nervous diseases. From this period dates the beginning of psychoanalysis.

Freud is rightly described as the founder of the psychoanalytic school of psychology. The term psychoanalysis refers both to a technique by which patients may be treated over a period of time, and also to the set of ideas or the theory underlying the technique. It is in the second sense that we shall use it in this chapter.

Four years after Freud established himself in private practice he married Martha Bernays, and what Freud jokingly referred to as the beginning of the thirty years' war proved in fact to be the start of over fifty happy years together. He was never a prosperous man and often had to face unpopularity because of his theories, but he worked very hard, treating patients during the day and writing prolifically in his spare time. The family had to flee from Vienna in 1938 when Hitler's armies invaded Austria. Freud had often wished to live in England, and it is therefore somewhat ironical that he should die there in 1939 after sixteen years of suffering from cancer of the jaw.

The nature of personality

Freud lived at a time when there was even more self-deception than there is today, and it might be true to claim that the change is in part due to him. There is now a wider realization that men are not so rational in their arguments nor so objective in their judgments as was once believed. The ideas underlying such Freudian concepts as rationalization and projection are frequently encountered, even if the terms themselves are seldom heard. Freud has to some degree succeeded in convincing man of his irrationality.

He has done this by stressing the importance of unconscious motivation, by drawing our attention to the fact that there are a number of things we do for which we can give no explanation. Freud believed that the key to understanding these inexplicable aspects of behaviour is the unconscious mind. By means of hypnosis the motives could be recovered and brought into consciousness—Freud had learned this through his encounter with Charcot, and initially he used this method of treating his patients. In the unconscious mind hidden motives, complexes (ideas heavily charged with emotion) and buried memories are stored, and since they are unconscious special methods must be used to bring them to light: psychoanalysis is the name given to Freud's particular method.

Freud considered the unconscious mind very important.

It has been likened to that much larger part of a floating iceberg which remains submerged and invisible. The conscious is the smaller part which is in contact with the environment; it is represented by the individual's present mental state—what one is thinking about at the moment in question. Is everything else then part of the unconscious? Freud realized that there are things of which we may not be thinking at the moment but which could very readily be summoned into consciousness, for example, our address or date of birth. Such 'memories' are not unconscious but represent mental states which Freud called preconscious. Unlike unconscious memories, they can be recalled at will. Even unconscious memories however remain accessible to certain methods: hypnosis can enable us to recall things that happened in babyhood and even before birth. According to Freud, nothing is ever forgotten. Recent work on the physiological basis of memory suggests Freud may well be right in this respect, memories being coded within particular brain cells rather than in traces between them which deteriorate over a period of time if not used.

Freud found, in using the technique of psychoanalysis, that there was often considerable resistance to the bringing of repressed trouble-causing ideas into consciousness. Somehow the repressed idea was not permitted to surface. This led him to reformulate his theory of mental structure.

Personality, he claimed, is made up of three systems interacting so closely that it is barely possible to disentangle them. These are the *Id*, the *Ego* and the *Superego*.

The first of these, and ontogenetically the oldest, is the Id. Crudely expressed, this is the mind of the baby, the biological substratum of behaviour. It is necessarily self-centred and it works so as to maximize pleasure and to minimize pain, its prime function being to relieve the tensions that arise. So as to obtain pleasure and avoid pain, the Id has two processes by which it can work: the first consists of reflex actions such as sneezing or blinking when some discomfort affects the nose or eyes; the second lies in a capacity to form mental pictures or images to help fulfil its desires. Thus the hungry person has a mental picture of food, an image which in part fulfils the desire and which is therefore called a wish-fulfilment, but it cannot fully deal with the tension set up by the hunger, so some process of interacting with the environment must be established. This secondary process is what Freud calls the Ego.

Because the Id is selfish and demanding, and because its demands are excessive, the Ego has to mediate between the Id and the environment, to modify the Id's demands in accordance with what is available. It must persuade the Id to accept the limitations of the environment and so maintain an appearance of respectability. The Ego is the facet of the personality which the rest of society sees and interacts with. To preserve his reputation, a person must appear to be law-abiding and respectable, not dominated by the primitive passions of the Id.

The Superego has been described as the moral arm of the personality. Whereas the Id operates according to the *pleasure principle* of maximizing pleasure and minimizing pain, the Superego aims at perfection; it seeks to do more than merely postpone the gratification of the desires of the Id—its aim is to deny, limit or transform such gratification. People have equated the Superego with conscience; indeed, both are formed in much the same way by the introjection of parental vetoes, and both restrain behaviour, but the Superego consists not only of a restraining conscience but also of an ego-ideal or image of the self as it ought to be, this image having been built up out of the elements of behaviour rewarded by the parents. The Superego has a threefold function: it must inhibit the primitive impulses of the Id since these are disapproved of by society; it must attempt to raise the aspirations of the Ego to moral goals rather than merely realistic ones; and it must strive for perfection. Like the Id, the Superego is largely non-rational, but, unlike the Id, it is the product of socialization—its strength depends on the social environment in which it develops. The Id is the biological component of personality and the Superego the social component.

The Id and the Superego will necessarily clash with each other and the Ego must find a way of mediating between them and of trying to satisfy both of them, at least in part: it wants to allow the Id as much freedom as possible without upsetting the Superego. Where a painful repressed memory is struggling to re-enter consciousness and a strong Superego holds it back, the struggles may be so prolonged and intense as to cause breakdown. Psychoanalysis, as a form of therapy, must therefore be a permissive process, complete freedom of expression being allowed, all the barriers usually erected by society being down. Allowing some of the inadmissible impulses and ideas of the Id to rise to the surface and be accepted at a conscious level may be one way of dealing with them.

The workings of personality

Freudian theory rests on the twin pillars of *repression* and *infantile sexuality*. The latter will be briefly described in the next section. The former, the process of repression, is frequently an underlying feature of mental disturbance. Ideas which would cause the individual pain are unwittingly thrust out of consciousness and lie deep in the unconscious. It is important to note that these trouble-causing ideas are not consciously denied; this would amount to suppressing them. Repression is an unconscious process, giving the individual absolute sincerity in being unable to recognize his repressions as part of his experience. They are not allowed to re-enter consciousness but they may trouble the conscious mind in some disguised way, for example, by compelling a person to perform certain actions or to believe certain things. Such repressed memories or ideas may cause distress, which is converted into physical symptoms such as a paralysed arm, blindness, deafness or loss of speech. They may cause the personality to become dissociated so that the individual becomes two or three different 'persons'. Such a case is described in the book, subsequently filmed, *Three Faces of Eve* (Thigpen and Cleckley, 1957): a woman develops three quite different personalities because of a traumatic event in early childhood, a painful memory which had been repressed.

One of the ways in which repressed ideas seek expression is shown in the psychoneurotic disorders, but they may also seek expression through our dreams. We noted above, in discussing the Id, that the primary process seeks to bring pleasure by forming images of desired objects. This may happen during sleep, and Freud regards dreaming as a means of wish-fulfilment. It would be a mistake to assume that all dreams express repressed wishes and fears—some are quite obviously connected with the events and problems of the previous day and Freud openly admits this—but some clearly demonstrate the struggles of the Id. Freud's first book was *The Interpretation of Dreams*, written in 1900, a work of which he remained proud throughout his life. Because the dream has a wish-fulfilling aim and because direct revelation of the desires of the Id would be so disturbing as to cause the sleeper to waken, the dreams must be disguised. The process of dream-work therefore translates the *latent content* of the dream into the *manifest content*, and the task of interpretation involves moving back from what is actually dreamed to the

19

desires underlying it. The objects in the dream are symbols. Thus the man who dreams repeatedly of missing a train may be the man who is eager to get ahead but constantly dreads failure. Freud made extensive use of dream analysis as part of his treatment because of his belief in dreams as 'the royal road to the unconscious'.

It is from the unconscious that the psychic energy which drives the individual emanates. This energy is called the *libido*. At first it was thought to be of a sexual nature, and it was because of Freud's emphasis on sex as the mainspring of behaviour that some of his early disciples forsook him. Later he widened his concept of libidinal energy so that it came to approximate to the hedonistic craving or desire of the Buddhist religion. The most important point about libidinal energy in considering how personality works is that it is displaceable, that is to say, it may be deflected from one unattainable goal-object to another one: if an unmarried woman has a strong desire for children, she may in part satisfy this desire by becoming a teacher. If the energy cannot find expression in one way, it must find a substitute way. It has been likened to crude oil gushing out of the earth and able to be refined or transformed according to needs and circumstances (Stafford-Clark, 1967). Alternatively it may be thought of as being like electricity in that the same energy may be used for heat, light or driving a motor.

Psychic energy or libido, emanating from the Id, aims at the reduction of tension. Indeed, in *Beyond the Pleasure Principle*, published in 1920, Freud suggests that man's most basic drive is to return to the quiescent state in which he was before the action of cosmic forces on inorganic matter brought about his creation as man; the ideal tensionless state would be the stability of the inorganic world. This unconscious death-wish (thanatos) cannot be satisfied, so the aggressive feelings are turned outwards, and show

20

themselves in negative behaviour such as hating, killing and avoiding. The other main drive is directed towards self-preservation and is the sex drive (eros) used in the wide sense referred to above.

The Ego, in trying to moderate the cravings of the Id in terms of reality, has a difficult task. It is attacked by many anxieties: about dangers in the environment, about powerful instincts that may get out of control, about flouting the dictates of the Superego. The Ego must find a way of coping with so much anxiety. Truly rational ways are not always possible, so, in self-defence, the Ego must find other non-rational ways. These are known as *defence mechanisms*.

Libidinal energy is repeatedly frustrated and has to be displaced. Because of the clash between the desires of the Id and the demands of society, substitute goals must frequently be found. The emotion accompanying the forbidden desire to punch the boss on the nose is expressed in beating the wife. Scapegoating of this kind is a common way of displacing aggressive feelings on to an innocent victim.

Sometimes the primitive desire may be refined and turned into something much more respectable; when this happens, the desire is said to have been sublimated. Where a sexual outlet is denied, the individual thus frustrated may find some relief in composing music or lyrical poetry or engaging in religious activities. Freud claimed that the Madonnas painted by Leonardo have their origin in the painter's early separation from his mother and the frustration of his longed-for intimacy with her. Lofty achievements in the world of art have, in Freud's view, very lowly origins: sexual impulses have contributed invaluably to the highest cultural, artistic and social achievements of the human mind. Unfortunately a substitute, however good, is never as satisfying as the real thing and the tension is not completely released. This is why our society is so discontented; it is the price paid for being civilized. We are restless because some libidinal energy remains unused and drives us hither and thither in an attempt to deal with the tension in a socially acceptable way.

The Ego is anxious because the Id may get out of hand, or the Superego, like the prudish aunt, may be offended by its behaviour. It is also anxious about difficulties in the external world, but this third kind of anxiety is preferable to the others. The Ego can defend itself therefore by turning neurotic and moral anxiety into what Freud calls reality anxiety. Hating another person is hardly respectable and it may well lead to the Id's getting out of hand; it is easier to turn this anxiety into anxiety about something in the real world—by believing for example that one is hated by the other person. Thus, 'I hate him' becomes 'He hates me', and this is a much more tolerable state of affairs. Moral anxiety, caused by a troublesome Superego, may be converted into a feeling that it is someone in the real world who is the persecutor. The reproaches of conscience about one's own stinginess may turn into a belief that it is other people who are stingy. One investigation showed that people who were rated by others as being high in stinginess assigned higher than average stinginess scores to others. If one despises oneself, one may very soon come to believe others despise one. Aggressive people believe it is others who are the aggressive ones. We tend, as Christ put it, to see the mote in our brother's eye before we notice the beam in our own.

It is important to realize that these *projections*, as Freud called them, are unconscious; most people do not realize when they are projecting. But it has been found that those who have little insight into or understanding of themselves tend to project more than do those who know themselves better. In fact it seems to the writer that simply to know that one is liable to project one's attitudes and feelings on to other people makes one more cautious in making judgments about them. If we would know other people accurately, we must first know ourselves.

Piaget has shown that the child has great difficulty in distinguishing between ideas in his mind and objects and events in the external world. What is subjective and what is objective are often confused. Even adults are not free from such confusions; their interpretation of the external world is strongly influenced by their subjective moods. Hungry people looking at blurred coloured shapes see them as food. Happy people recognize words fitting in with their present mood more quickly than other words. Aspects of our current mental states are projected on to our environment. The girl who is very eager to have a suitor believes men do actually chase her through the park on her way home from work. Like the dream, projection may sometimes operate so as to fulfil our wishes.

Another way the Ego defends itself is by replacing the impulse that is causing anxiety by its opposite. If we dislike another person, we may either believe it is he who dislikes us (projection) or we may make excessively friendly overtures to him to compensate for our true feelings. On the other hand, the girl who loves a boy but, for one reason or another, dare not let it be known, may appear cold and hostile towards him. The person who is afraid of the power of his or her sex drive may appear very prudish and be shocked at anything that smacks, even faintly, of sensuality. The very gentle person may be compensating for his real sadism. The excessively confident man may be at heart a coward with strong feelings of inferiority. In the words of W. S. Gilbert, 'Things are seldom what they seem', and the presence of these *over-compensations* and *reaction-formations* makes the interpretation of overt behaviour very difficult. How can real affection,

23

for example, be distinguished from reactive affection? Freud claimed that the criterion is extravagant showiness or protesting too much. The mother who grants her child's every wish may be compensating for the lack of genuine warm feeling she has for him. She does more than simply remove the defect; she over-compensates for it.

Everyone is aware of the way people rationalize their motives; this is another defence mechanism. If we do not wish to do a particular task, we invent reasons why we should not do it, and, what is more, we actually believe these to be the real reasons. We forget that where there is a will there is usually a way, and we search for arguments to justify us in believing what we want to believe or doing what we want to do. *Rationalization* amounts to self-deception: it is a protective barrier against the uncomfortable truth. A man alights from a bus without paying and deals with his guilt feelings by telling himself the bus company owed it to him as he had to stand all the way. The teacher who is afraid of appearing foolish before his pupils says he has not the time to be in the school pantomime or to play in the school-v.-staff hockey match. The girl whose boy-friend has jilted her persuades herself that he was not worth having anyway. This making of excuses by which we deceive even ourselves is extremely common.

Akin to this is the *restriction of the Ego*. Everyone hates to be a failure. It follows that if one does not attempt to do something one cannot fail in that activity. We special-ize in a particular academic subject so that, for example, if someone asks us to translate a phrase of Greek, we can unashamedly explain our inability to do so by claiming to be physicists or mathematicians. We should feel very ashamed if we had to admit to being classicists in these circumstances. By restricting itself, the Ego erects a barrier against failure.

Anxiety can be intolerably painful. Where the anxiety is

24

so extreme that it cannot be dealt with in the ways mentioned above, it may be repressed—thrust out of consciousness—and converted into a physical symptom. This may defend the Ego by giving the individual a legitimate excuse for not doing what he is afraid of doing: an attack of nausea or a splitting headache may save the face of the public speaker whose nervousness prevents him from turning up at the meeting; this is much better than losing face by giving an inadequate speech. Strange as it seems, the mind hands over the distress to the body, making it easier to bear and more likely to elicit sympathy.

These are a few of the ways in which the vulnerable Ego defends itself. They are very common, and they certainly provide ample evidence of the irrationality of man.

How personality develops

Freud shocked public opinion by drawing attention to the sexuality of the baby. The Id being the original personality, the baby is driven by libidinal energy expressing itself in all kinds of appetites and desires. As the libido develops, it passes through various stages when it centres in turn on different bodily areas. Pleasurable feelings during the first year are derived from the activities of sucking and taking in food: the mouth is therefore the first *erogenous zone* and this stage is called the *oral* period. Subsequently the anus and later still the genitals become the primary erogenous zones.

It is important to note that the way a child is handled during the oral, anal and phallic stages of his development determines his adult personality. Transition from one stage to another is linked with anxiety, and if the anxiety is too great the individual may become fixated at a particular stage. This may be temporary or it may be permanent. If an adult has been fixated for a time at a particular stage

25

in childhood, he may, when confronted with intense anxiety, regress to the childish behaviour associated with that stage.

Regression may also occur in children when they are frustrated. In one well-known experiment (Barker *et al.*, 1941) constructive play was observed in children. The children were then given more attractive toys to play with. The third stage was the lowering of a transparent screen between the children and the more attractive toys. When their play with the original toys was observed after this frustrating experience it was seen to be much less constructive. Their behaviour had regressed to a more childish level. In another investigation, performance on the Stanford-Binet Intelligence Scale was shown to be less good after a frustrating experience, showing that the boys involved had regressed to a lower level of mental functioning. The behaviour of the four-year-old child into whose home a baby brother or sister is brought is an example of regression commonly seen. Unemployed men with families to support may be driven by their anxiety to behave in childish and irresponsible ways.

Mention should be made of the *Oedipus complex* which Freud regarded as one of his greatest discoveries. During the phallic stage (3 to 5 years) the boy falls in love with his mother, as did Oedipus in the Greek story from which Freud borrowed the name, and regards his father as a rival. However, he fears his father's strength and is anxious lest he should be castrated by him. Repression of sexual desire for his mother and of hostility for his father is the way this anxiety is dealt with. Identification with the father then ensues, though the boy's attitude towards his father is likely to remain ambivalent: he both hates and admires him.

The oral, anal and phallic stages are called the pregenital stages. They are followed by what Freud called the *latency period*. During this period the impulses are in a state of repression, only to re-assert themselves at adolescence, when they are displaced or sublimated so that maturity can be attained.

It was stated above that personality develops largely as the result of displacements or *cathexes*. To be acceptable in society, libidinal energy must be rightly directed. The closer the substitute goal resembles the original one, the more it succeeds in releasing tension. If one substitute becomes unattainable, another displacement must occur and so on. Choice of substitute depends on two factors: (1) how far the substitute is socially acceptable, and (2) how far it resembles the original object-choice. What is socially acceptable is learned from the parents and other authority figures, and it is their restraints and injunctions that go to form the Superego. The process of internalizing these restraints and injunctions Freud called *introjection*.

Another process important in personality development is known as *identification*. Here, the qualities of an external object, usually a person, are incorporated into one's personality; they become part of oneself. The boy identifies with his father because the latter is more successful and stronger than he is; later he identifies with other 'heroes' who are able to gratify their needs more than he can his. It is important to note that most identification is unconscious; it goes much deeper than conscious copying. It operates so as to reduce tension, and the more successful it is in doing this, the stronger the identification will be.

The child with parents who reject him may reduce his tension by identifying with them, hoping thereby to regain their love. If a loved parent has died, a child may reduce his sense of loss by incorporating features of the parent's personality within his own. Probably the most influential

27

identifications are those made with the parents, but one's final personality is influenced by the numerous identifications made through its development.

Freud attached enormous importance to the early years of life. These are the decisive years for personality development, the formative years. He claimed that the essential foundations of character are laid down by the time the child is three, and these established traits may be modified but not radically altered by later events. When we consider the rate at which intelligence is developing and social learning progressing during this period, Freud's claim seems very plausible.

More doubts have been expressed about his contention that the cause of neurotic breakdown may almost invariably be found in the intimate domestic events of early childhood. Jung held, for instance, that a present neurosis must have a cause which is itself in the present. Freud, however, based his claim on the reconstructed past lives of the neurotic patients who consulted him in Vienna; in almost every case, the psychoanalytic technique revealed some decisive event in early childhood.

In summary, the Id, the storehouse of instinctual drives present at birth, needs an agent to interact with the environment so the Ego emerges. Introjection of social restraints and ideals leads the Superego to develop to prevent the Id from getting out of hand. Libidinal energy is changed and refined to fit in with the demands of society. The Ego finds ways of dealing with besetting anxieties whilst keeping up the appearance of respectability and attempting to bring about some integration within the personality.

An evaluation of Freud's theory

Despite the fact that many laymen still think of psychology and Freud's theories as being roughly synonymous, the status of Freud within present-day academic psychology in Britain is not high. In some circles, he is considered of merely historical interest—tolerated, even valued, as an example of how misguided psychology is without the guidance of scientific methods. His impact, however, has been considerable. What tends to happen is that the ideas of a psychologist in time become absorbed into the fabric of psychological knowledge and one loses sight of their originator. As a case in point, the psychology of Jung is often omitted from university courses in psychology, yet his influence can be clearly detected in the writings of some contemporary psychologists.

What are the reasons for Freud's unpopularity with academic psychologists? Three reasons will be suggested here.

Freud introduced new personality constructs as he discovered new information in treating his patients. Considering the wide scope of his theory, it is surprising how few these are. However, it is argued by Freud's critics that the relationships between the constructs used to explain personality are often not made clear. What, for example, is the connection between the Oedipus complex and the Superego? The theory stands accused of being disjointed and ambiguous: a number of important questions remain unanswered, and some of its terms lack clarity of definition. This is a valid criticism so far as the goodness of the theory *qua* theory goes, but certain of Freud's basic constructs, such as repression, still constitute one effective foundation for the understanding of human behaviour. Even if the total theory appears lacking in coherence, parts of the theory are psychologically useful.

Another valid criticism of Freud's theory as he left it is that it paid too little attention to the cultural determinants of personality. As Gorer (1966) points out in his essay on

29

'Psychoanalysis in the world', only once in all his writings does Freud admit the possibility of character's being modified by culture. Yet consider the case of the Oedipus complex. Though, as Jones (1953) points out, the Oedipal situation is universal, anthropologists have shown that the particular form it takes depends on the prevailing pattern of family structure. The form it takes in western cultures, for instance, is related to the father's dominant position in the family. Erik Erikson (1963), using case-studies of people living in very different circumstances, demonstrates how the Ego's development is closely bound up with the organization of society. Freud would have to concede that this is so to a much greater extent than he admitted.

Perhaps the main reason for Freud's unpopularity is that psychology, like the Ego, must preserve its respectability, and that means being scientific. To be acceptable in a world of science, psychology must use empirical methods: it must proceed by putting speculation to experimental test and its findings must be publicly observable.

The scientific approach to the study of behaviour began in the last century with the establishment of the first psychological laboratory in Germany. Freud came under the influence of Wundt, the man regarded as the first experimental psychologist, and of Fechner, the psychophysicist, but he declined to use experimental methods as the basis for his theories. There are no tables or graphs in Freud's writings. He does not seem to have considered the scientific approach appropriate for studying the human personality. He is even reported as having said that his theories were proved on the couch and had no need of experimental evidence.

This may sound like arrogance on Freud's part, and perhaps he was arrogant. There can be no doubting that he held his views very strongly. The Freudian theory has been accused of being quite without scientific foundation, yet it was based on accumulated evidence and is not simply a piece of armchair introspection and speculation. But, though one must acknowledge the existence of evidence, there are two major faults: (1) the evidence was drawn from a number of middle-class Viennese neurotics —hardly a random sample!—and from Freud's own self-analysis, and (2) his interpretations of human behaviour have the effect of seeming to be purely imaginative creations because they are so far in excess of what is publicly observable. His methods of recording interviews with patients were not beyond criticism: he did not write down their revelations there and then; he wrote his reports in the evening following the interview. Human memory is prone to distortion of the facts, and there is no reason to believe Freud's memory was an exception.

It is also true that, in compiling his evidence, Freud did not make use of other sources to corroborate what he discovered in the course of psychoanalytic interviews. Present-day psychological assessments use not only the individual's own statements but any information provided by near relatives or from other relevant documents such as, for example, school reports. It is surely valuable to have more than one line of evidence.

If we are to regard Freud's theory of personality as a scientific one, then it cannot rank very highly because it lacks an essential criterion of scientific theory—falsifiability. A scientific theory must be capable of being proved false. This is simply not the case with some aspects of Freudian theory: they are just not open to proof or disproof by experiment. How, for example, could one *prove* the existence of an unconscious death-wish? But it is a mistake to assume, as is the modern tendency, that only the procedures and discoveries of the physical sciences are intellectually respectable. A theory may be respectable without being scientific (Farrell, 1970). Some truths come from sources other than science, and Freud's critics may not be making so stringent a criticism as it at first appears when they argue that Freudianism is more like a religious belief than a scientific theory.

Certainly some of Freud's followers appear to have deified him and taken too much on trust, but this is not Freud's fault. As Gorer (1966) points out, many psychoanalysts since Freud have, intentionally or otherwise, added to the popular layman's view of psychoanalysis as a kind of panacea. Discarding such extreme views, the writer believes that some of Freud's insights into the human personality are so penetrating that, until science discovers a means of testing them (which may well be impossible because of the limitations of science), they must be accepted for want of superior insights. We may not be so confident of the validity of the theory as Freud was; it may be more prudent to regard it as a series of hypotheses most of which are still to be tested, but working on the basis of an assumption may be regarded as better than total stagnation. Until one may know for certain, a working hypothesis is necessary. Psychology is not yet an exact science. Methods of testing and measurement need much more refinement. The psychologist must therefore choose his theoretical standpoint not because it is already conclusively proved but for other reasons.

What might these reasons be? First, there is the comprehensiveness of Freud's theory of personality: it has been described as a theory whose scope, unity and coherence are unmatched in psychology (Inkeles, 1963), though it may be true to say that psychoanalysis appears more comprehensive than it is because of the looseness and ambiguity of some of its concepts. Factual evidence may destroy parts of the theory, such as the universal nature of the Oedipal phase or the view of the dream as the guardian of sleep, but such parts are inessential, and the theory will

32

still have its adherents until a better, more comprehensive theory is proposed. Second, Freud's insights into some of the ways the mind works are very penetrating. Some have been confirmed by experimental studies (Sears, 1944). Freud opened men's eyes to some of their irrationalities. He showed the importance of unconscious motivation, though some, like Adler, Allport and Rogers, would maintain he overstated this. Third, parts of his theory have effectively generated research, and there is a school of thought which holds that this is more important than how 'good' the theory is. The theory of psychoanalysis, though some of its tenets are untestable, has inspired many investigations, and undoubtedly knowledge of human nature has advanced because of these.

Freud had so much confidence in his findings that he would rather lose his associates than change his views. He would not listen readily to his critics and clung to his ideas with an almost obsessional tenacity. If he had been less dogmatic, the breaks with Adler and Jung would almost certainly not have been so absolute.

On the other hand, Freud's mind was not completely closed, though he was slow to change. It must be remembered that he reformulated his theory of the structure of personality at least once during his lifetime. Doubtless other changes would have been made in the light of further insights. A brief summary of major developments in psychoanalytic theory since Freud's death follows in the next section.

Psychoanalysis since Freud

Since Freud's death in 1939 the theory of psychoanalysis has undergone a number of changes. Knowledge cannot afford to be static, and when Hebb (1949) says of theorizing that it is like skating on thin ice, he is right: one must keep moving or drown. The practice of psychoanalysis has stood the test of time: many of Freud's techniques are still used in psychotherapy. It is interesting that Freud himself claimed to foresee a time when all nervous disorders would be cured by administering chemical drugs without any psychological treatment. Much depends on what is meant by 'cure' however. For a discussion of this concept see Storr (1966).

Freud's theory has been developed along the following lines:

(1) In the development of personality, social relations have been stressed rather than biological factors. Erikson (1959), for example, whilst accepting Freud's psychosexual stages, suggests additional later stages, and regards the problem of how the individual adapts to the environment at the specific crisis associated with each stage as being more significant than the biological stages themselves. The way in which future crises are met is affected by the way in which each developmental crisis is resolved by parents or others, who themselves are strongly influenced by the particular culture. Freud's followers see the main source of conflict within the individual as the Ego's interaction with the external world, no longer the struggle between the Id and the Superego. The role of the instincts has certainly been played down. The death-instinct is widely discredited: studies of sensory deprivation (e.g. Vernon, 1965) have shown clearly that, far from enjoying the completely tensionless state, subjects deprived of all sensory bombardment have sought stimulation with increasing eagerness.

(2) The Ego has come to the fore in post-Freudian theory. Freud always regarded the Id as the dominant partner in personality throughout life: some of his followers, notably Hartmann (1958), have made the Ego autonomous.

34

It is important to guard against the danger of thinking of the Ego, the Id and the Superego as spectral realities within the person; they were conceived simply as an aid to understanding the workings of personality. What has happened since Freud is that a more adequate view of the relationship between conscious and unconscious processes has been developed.

(3) Linked with this growth in the importance of the Ego is the diminution of the importance of sex as a behaviour determinant. In the later development of Freudian theory during Freud's own lifetime there was a balance of emphasis on sex and aggression in the forms of love and hate. Freud realized that in his earlier theory the role of aggression had been seriously underestimated. He still saw the individual, however, as impelled by drives rather than attracted by goals. Adler and Jung did much to change this view of the individual (see chapter 4) and their influence on later psychoanalytic theories is apparent. Storr (1960) sees the aim of psychotherapy as self-actualization and the individual's goals as being equally important in diagnosis and treatment as the causes of his behaviour. Causes are of less relevance in considering human personality than motives which arise out of the current situation. Many modern psychoanalysts concentrate on the individual's present situation so as to show him that his early life experiences constitute a dynamic factor in his present state. Some, Laing (1960) for instance, acknowledge the influence on their thinking of existential philosophy. What is called *existential analysis*, inspired jointly by the work of Freud and the existentialists, is growing in importance in Western Europe after its recent rise to popularity in the United States. It is not within the scope of this chapter to discuss the theories of the existential analysts. It is enough to say that any theory of personality which totally ignores the influence of the past

is highly questionable. An account such as Erikson's (1959), which deals with the inter-relationship of past, present and future, seems altogether more satisfactory.

4

The Adlerian account of personality

Alfred Adler (1870-1937)

Partly because he was born fourteen years after Freud, Adler is often referred to as one of Freud's disciples. Even in the early days when he was a member of Freud's circle in Vienna Adler would never accept that he was a disciple; he thought of himself always as a colleague. Indeed in many ways Adler anticipated Freud rather than followed him.

He was born in a suburb of Vienna in 1870. His father was a prosperous corn merchant and both his parents were of Hungarian-Jewish extraction. Alfred was the second son in a family of six children. Certain incidents and relationships in his early life seem to have been important for the development of his theory of personality, so these must be mentioned here. He was a delicate child, suffering both from rickets and in early years from spasm of the glottis which placed him in danger of death by suffocation. Because of his ill health, his parents tended to pamper him. However, when his younger brother was born, his mother, according to Alfred, transferred most of her attention to the baby and he felt 'dethroned'; he turned to his father and always thereafter preferred him to his mother.

Alfred was his father's favourite, Leopold having great faith in his son's potentialities. He was a colourful personality, and accounts we have of relations with his family make interesting reading. Alfred's fondness for music and his love of the countryside both owe much to his early environment. Because he suffered from rickets, which made every movement an effort for him, he developed a conviction that life is movement. He envied his elder brother's agility and this may have been one of the reasons for the dislike he felt for him.

From the fourth year of his life, Alfred knew he wanted to be a doctor. When he was three, his younger brother died in a bed next to his, an event which must have made a searing impression on the sensitive and intelligent child. A year or so later he himself had pneumonia, and, having heard the doctor say to his father, 'Your son is lost', Alfred resolved that he would live to become a doctor himself. Some years later, however, his schoolmaster had other ideas. Alfred's mathematics was so poor that his teacher suggested he ought to leave school and become a cobbler—a remark which did little to boost his pupil's diminishing morale. Then one day the teacher was stumped by an arithmetical problem. Alfred, who had been working hard at home to overcome his difficulties, suddenly stood up and offered to solve the problem. Despite the teacher's sarcastic reaction, he did so, and from that day he became the best pupil in the mathematics class!

At the university Adler did excellent work, and in 1898 he set himself up in private practice. He had an excellent manner with his patients, probably born of his belief that if you wanted to be a good doctor you had to be a kind human being.

He met Freud at a meeting of the Viennese Society of Medicine. Freud had given a lecture which was received very unfavourably, much to Freud's annoyance. Adler
38

strongly supported what Freud had said, and was later invited to join Freud's discussion circle. He claims to have found these discussions inspiring, but in 1907, he published his first work on psychology, *Inferiority of Organs*, and in it a clear divergence from Freud became apparent. Adler ascribed some bad habits in children to faulty attempts to overcome the defective functioning of certain organs: Freud believed the source was always sexual. By 1910 the differences between Freud and Adler had become serious, and in 1911 Adler openly criticized Freud's sexual theory. Man for Adler was motivated by the urge for power, not by the desire for pleasure. The rift in 1911 marked the beginning of the Adlerian school of thought which has come to be known as Individual Psychology.

The nature of personality

In the course of a lifetime we make many statements, some of them not seriously meant. This is why we should be wrong in attaching too much importance to Freud's saying that he regarded mankind as 'trash' or to Adler's claim to love the music of a great street full of people moving about their daily business, and yet in some way these statements seem typical of the men who made them. Their attitudes to mankind were very different. Freud saw man as egotistical and hedonistic, basically anti-social: Adler saw him as altruistic and humanitarian, motivated primarily by social urges. *Social interest*, a key concept in Adler's theory, is innate, though its growth can be warped by an adverse environment, or rather by the child's interpretation of his environment. The first point to notice is that Adler saw human nature as basically good—the antithesis of Freud's view.

Adler presents us with no complex view of the structure of personality; he makes no attempt to divide it into

39

parts. The two vital concepts for Adler's theory are the *unity* of the personality and its *uniqueness*.

When Adler founded the school of Individual Psychology in 1912 he chose the name because he felt that it best expressed his view of man as a single, indivisible individual, that is to say, man as a unity. No single aspect of a man's behaviour could be considered in isolation from his whole personality. The whole scroll of the individual's life had to be unrolled in order to understand a single event. To use a musical metaphor, which Adler had a fondness for doing, the significance of a few notes cannot be understood if torn from the context of the whole melody. All expressions of personality are consistent parts of a whole, and the whole is unified because of the *style of life* the individual has chosen.

Adler believed Freud greatly overestimated the importance of the unconscious. As the years passed, the idea of unconscious drives satisfied him less and less, and that of conscious motives appealed more and more. This was the way his thought evolved. To speak of the conscious and unconscious mind as antagonists was to make a division in the unity of the personality which Adler could not countenance. The so-called unconscious really consisted of those parts of our consciousness which we could not understand; once they were understood they became part of consciousness.

The other important concept was the uniqueness of the personality. Adler was concerned with individuals, each one being different. He could not accept a theory of types similar to that of another early member of Freud's circle, Jung, who divided people, according to their dominant attitudes, into extraverted and introverted personalities. According to Adler, two introverted persons were never the same. To classify people into types was a scientific aid and nothing more. All it did was to abstract from the individual some of his many traits so as to compare them with traits abstracted in an equally arbitrary way from other individuals. Likenesses were accentuated, differences overlooked, and the result was a completely distorted picture of the individual drawn up to fit into a particular scheme. This view of typologies in personality theories is highly consonant with Allport's contention that so long as a theory deals with universals, it will not deal with the human personality. The latter is individual and unique.

Style of life has been mentioned above. This idea is very important in Adler's theory: indeed it has been referred to as the theory's slogan (Hall and Lindzey, 1957). Certainly, considering the nature of an individual's personality, his style of life is the major component: Adler even went so far as to equate style of life with the whole personality or the self. It is based on the individual's unique interpretation of life, and it gives consistency and unity to his thought and behaviour. Man creates his style of life through his reactions to life's circumstances, and the style so created determines the way in which man subsequently satisfies his needs and deals with his impulses. We shall keep returning to this concept in the sections which follow.

The workings of personality

Man's nature is not an inevitable consequence of his life history. It is not what happened to him at some past time which makes him what he is now. This was one of the issues on which Freud and Adler increasingly disagreed. For Adler, man is directed from before, not impelled from behind. He is motivated by goals and ideals present now as ideas in his mind leading him to press forward towards their attainment in reality.

He is not the helpless victim of the past; nor is he at the mercy of strong biological drives in the present. The drives are there, but how man is affected by them depends on the style of life he has adopted. His sexual drives do not determine his style of life, as Freud would have it: this, for Adler, was putting the cart before the horse. The style of life is formed long before the sex drive becomes pressing in the life of the individual, and it will therefore determine how this drive is dealt with. Adler pointed out to his readers the danger of paying attention to those who stress the importance of sex in motivation: he could see no reason for placing 'this unnatural emphasis' on that particular function (1929). A much more important drive was aggression, but even this did not determine the individual's behaviour. It could only influence him in ways consistent with his style of life. Socially determined attitudes were much more important than biological drives.

Adler had approached psychology through his work in general medicine; he had approached the mind through the body, and he appreciated the closeness of the relationship between the two. He regarded the body, not simply as a mechanical collection of cells, but as a purposive organism: all its parts work together towards wholeness or help. The natural aim of the body was the repairing and strengthening of itself, and, where there was weakness, the compensation for that deficiency, as when the chronically weak heart enlarges itself to cope with its work. Mental processes worked in a similar way. Where there was a physical weakness, the individual's attention became riveted on it and there followed a psychic striving to overcome the deficiency. This sometimes led to successes far greater than were found in people without such weaknesses. As an example, a child born with a weak respiratory system and related speech problems, struggles to communicate his needs; he is praised for his small successes, so he struggles more and goes from strength to strength. Through repeated successes he ends by becoming an actor of some repute. The organ inferiority which he had made him start the strivings which took him to the heights of success; without this inferiority the effort would probably not have been made. Imperfection of the organ may be the spur to great achievement because of the special effort it generates. There are many famous examples: Demosthenes, the great orator of the ancient world, was afflicted by a stammer—he fought to overcome it by standing on the shore, filling his mouth with pebbles and shouting down the waves; Beethoven, Mozart and Bruckner all had defects of the ear in childhood, yet all became eminent musicians; Schiller, Daudet, Homer and Milton each had some eye defect, yet their writings are strong in visual imagery; Byron was lame but became a notable swimmer. The examples are too numerous to be purely coincidental. The organ inferiority and the striving to overcome it provides the key.

However, not all short-sighted people become writers showing acute powers of observation; not all children with speech defects become actors or orators. It is not the physical defect itself which is important psychologically, but the child's attitude towards it. The objective fact matters little; what does matter is the way his experience of it affects him. It is his subjective view of it that is significant in forming his life-style. Some children are defeated by it and become pessimistic: others resolve to overcome it. Doubtless they are helped or hindered by the attitudes of those around them.

Physical attributes which are not defects in a medical sense may also affect personality development because of the child's attitude to them. Red hair may lead to a boy's being teased and the boy may develop difficult behaviour. Small stature may lead boys to test themselves against taller companions, thus becoming more combative than average.

Many small men have become military leaders, for example, Napoleon, Wellington and Nelson. Children who are ugly have great problems to contend with because of social prejudice. They may easily come to feel unwanted, and this may lead to anti-social behaviour and eventually crime. Adler draws attention to the fact that criminals are often strikingly ugly men. The left-handed child also is at a disadvantage in a world arranged to suit right-handed persons; he may develop a sense of failure which may need careful handling. (Modern research has shown that attempts to make a left-handed child right-handed have led to stuttering and that left-handed children have a greater than average chance of becoming delinquent.) People who are members of a minority population or a dissenting religious sect may be influenced by such membership: Jews and Quakers have often become successful in life, perhaps because of the special efforts they have had to make.

We are all driven by the will to succeed, the desire for superiority. It is seen clearly, according to Adler, in every psychological phenomenon, being an intrinsic necessity of life itself. It is innate and a part of life. It may show itself in hundreds of different ways, normally of a social nature, but this striving for superiority is the prepotent motive in human life.

In a social climate where for generations women have been regarded as inferior, it is not surprising that the ideas of masculinity and superiority should come to be closely associated, as well as those of femininity and inferiority. Out of this situation arises the masculine protest, the striving to be a man. It seemed to Adler that in our culture every woman wanted to be a man. Women show this desire when they choose a profession such as engineering, normally the domain of the male, or when they develop men's interests or wear clothes which are traditionally

44

masculine. Men also show the masculine protest whenever they evince a defensive reaction against being the underdog. (Adler might have found it hard to account for the apparent inversion of the masculine protest shown in the men who grow their hair long and sport perms and perfumes!)

Everyone strives for the goal of superiority, but there are countless ways of doing this. Depending on the inferiority we are attempting to compensate for, we may resolve to become superior through physique or intellect or in some other way: the goal we choose determines our style of life. All our behaviour will spring from this particular goal: everything we do will be with an eye to its attainment.

Because of this fact, a person's behaviour is a source of many clues to his life-style. His particular likes and dislikes, the heroes he admires, the job ambitions he has during childhood all tell us something about his goal of superiority. The way the person enters the room, shakes hands, smiles and walks all reflect his life-style. Whilst aware of the need for caution in interpretation, Adler suggested that the way a person stands may be indicative, especially if his stance is exaggerated in some way. If he stands excessively straight, it may be assumed that he feels much less great than he wants to appear; a bent stance may denote cowardice. Adler anticipates some of the modern work on social interaction in his suggestion that the distance at which the client sits from the interviewer may reveal a good deal. Even the posture a person adopts in sleeping may be a clue to his life-style: lying stretched out full length on the back is a sign that he wants to appear great; curling up under the bedclothes may show a lack of courage, and sleeping on the stomach suggests a negative and obstinate nature (1929).

Not only overt behaviour but fantasies, dreams and

memories are of value in understanding personality. Adler saw fantasy as an open door through which we may glimpse the workshop of the mind (1939). What the individual imagines to be true is of much more significance than his objective situation. Likewise what he remembers from his early life is more significant than all the things that actually happened to him then. His memories represent his 'story of my life'—a story which keeps reminding him of his goal, since what he remembers will never run counter to his style of life. His earliest memories will show this style of life as it begins to form : what he remembers must be of great importance to him, and if we know what is of most importance to him we know his goal and his life-style.

Dreams provide clues to personality because they denote the individual's attitudes to life. Freud saw the dream as emanating from the past; Adler saw it as pointing forward to the problems of the future. The dream is not a wish-fulfilment but a rehearsal for action : it leaves certain feelings behind and these push us forward towards the solution of our problems. Herein lies its value. It is interesting how the content of dreams changes during treatment, often showing an improvement in the patient's attitude towards the presenting problem.

How personality develops

Soon after Adler dissociated himself from Freud's circle, he was influenced by the writings of Hans Vaihinger who, in a book called *The Philosophy of 'As If'* (1925), proposed that man guides his life by many fictional ideas which have no counterpart in reality. He simply accepts these fictions for their personal utility and discards them when their usefulness has disappeared. Adler came to believe that these fictions were very influential on an individual's conduct: one of them, an unrealizable ideal, may become a man's final goal, and his behaviour will be explainable in terms of this object of his strivings.

The final goal will obviously affect his choices and therefore the self or personality he creates. It is obviously closely bound up with the style of life he acquires. The important question to be considered in this section is: how does the life-style develop?

The first point to make is that it is formed very early in childhood, indeed by the time the child is four or five. It is clearly influenced by the inferiorities the child rightly or wrongly feels himself to have. This feeling of inferiority is universal; to have it is part of what it means to be a human being. One's life-style is an attempt to compensate for one's particular inferiority. Thus if one feels oneself to be a physical weakling, one's life-style will consist largely in doing those things which promote physical strength: Napoleon was small, hence the conquering spirit which characterized his life-style.

However, although some of his followers wished to accept this simple explanation as the whole one, Adler in his later work showed that there were other important factors in the formation of the life-style. Attitudes to inherited, often physical, characteristics were important but they were not all. The environment, especially the family, played a part.

Any account of personality development must consider the relative importance of heredity and environment, either explicitly or implicitly. Some psychologists hold one of these to be all-important, the other having little effect. Adler pays equal attention to both. One's personality is not determined by one's heredity nor by one's environment—to concede this would be to accept a causal explanation of personality. Man is free to create his own personality, and his *attitudes* to both hereditary and

47

environmental accidents are the raw materials of the creative self.

Imitation plays a part. We do not inherit traits of character such as dishonesty, insolence or incompetence in arithmetic. These appear to run in families, but this is because of imitation; we identify with others and copy one another, often without realizing it. This may even apply to psychosomatic conditions. Adler tells of one of his patients who had a rash which she claimed to have inherited from her mother. Certainly her mother had the same kind of skin trouble. One might have believed the heredity story had not the mother disclosed to Adler that her daughter was adopted. Thus even a physical condition such as a non-infectious rash had been copied from a parent: it had got the mother out of some difficulties, why not the daughter?

The environment influences personality development not by its objective nature but by the child's interpretation or evaluation of it. Parents often believe they have given their offspring the same treatment but no two children in any family ever receive this because what they receive will be seen differently by each child. Adler points out that there are as many environments as there are individuals experiencing them; they exist not as outside facts but as they affect their perceivers. Our view of what happens to us is of necessity coloured by our life-style.

Position in the family has much to do with the way our personality develops. The family is like a constellation, father and mother being the sun and moon, the children being grouped around like stars. From the point of view of each star, the constellation looks different depending on its position. It is exactly the same with each child.

There are five well-defined types of child. The eldest has for a time been the only star. When the second arrived he was dethroned. This experience could lead either to resentment persisting throughout life or to a withdrawing of affection for the mother and possibly turning to the father. (In Adler's own childhood he had a good deal of affection and attention because of his physical weaknesses, but when other siblings were born and he had to share his mother's attention, he turned to his father who became the preferred parent.) The eldest child commonly identifies with the father because of his experience of dethronement. He becomes an upholder of family conventions, the conservative member of the family. The second child may be envious of the responsibilities given to the eldest and may therefore try to gain some other advantage over him. Thus if the first-born follows family tradition, the second may diverge in some striking way, for example, a member of a very artistic family may opt to become a soldier. Because of his inferior position in the family, he longs to surpass his rival; the older sibling is a pacemaker for him. The eldest looks back to the golden age of early childhood when he was the sole star; the second is oriented towards a brighter future. (It is interesting that Adler, himself a second child, emphasizes the striving for superiority.)

The youngest child in the family, because he is the smallest, desires to be the leader of all. Joseph dreamed that the other stars bowed down before his star; he was at that time the youngest child and his attitude typifies this position in the family.

The only child often appears precocious because he is accustomed largely to the society of adults. Because he is likely to be over-protected and because competition with siblings is not part of his early experience, he comes to view the world as a very unsheltered place, and he may as an adult seek a sheltered occupation such as that of a don or a clergyman.

The neglected child is the fifth clearly defined type. Dethronement has probably figured prominently in his early life, through death or divorce and remarriage of parents. His attitudes become ruthless and he seems to believe nothing will come to him unless he plots and fights to gain it. It is of course true that a large proportion of delinquents come from the background of the typical neglected child.

Adler stressed that it is not the objective family situation which leads to a particular life-style. It is the way in which the child experiences and evaluates the situation. Nor is it simply the order of birth that matters. Attitudes will be different if, say, the eldest child has some very serious handicap so that the second has to take on the lawgiver role, or if there is a gap of many years between one child and the next—a late-born child may be more like an only than a youngest. The situation in the family is important as well as the order of birth.

Although the family constellation is of the greatest significance in the development of the life-style, society as a whole also has some influence. The traditions of the environing culture have much to do with the differential development of boys and girls. Society expects men to show courage and independence so boys develop these traits. Different, often less desirable, characteristics are expected of women. Society expects girls to be weaker at mathematics: though they are not innately so, they come to believe this about themselves and so there are fewer eminent female mathematicians. The role which men and women have traditionally played in the division of labour obviously influences the developing life-style.

In *Social Interest* (1939) Adler suggests that there are three major problems of adaptation in life: we must adapt to life within the community, to work and to love. Each individual must solve, to his own satisfaction, these three problems which constantly confront him. They are inter-linked and the solving of one will often help solve another. Nor must one necessarily solve them in the usual way: thus a celibate monk may not satisfy the problem of love as most do through marriage but he may feel no sense of failure in respect of this problem: it is the *feeling* of failure to adapt that matters. If one can square oneself with these three demands of life to one's own satisfaction and in accordance with social interest or to the benefit of society one is immune from neurosis; failure to do so makes neurotic breakdown probable. Obviously these three prob-lems of adaptation confront the adult more forcibly than they do the child, but their satisfactory resolution is a prerequisite of wholesome personality development.

An evaluation of Adler's theory

Adler's theory of personality strikes one as sound common sense. This is the initial impression it makes and this may account for its immense popularity in the twenties and thirties. It was more palatable than Freud's theory—sex was put in its proper place—and there is less of a mystique about it, no mysterious and sinister Id and death-wish. Indeed Adler seems, more especially in his later works, to be holding a friendly chat with his readers. There are those who, largely because of the common sense it seems to abound in, say that Adler's theory is superficial. The writer rejects this view. Certain truths about human nature are often so obvious that they are unrecognized until made explicit: Adler's point about the environment is a good example—very few people appreciate that it is the way the environment is perceived by the individual that is significant rather than the objective situation. When this fact is grasped it seems like common sense, but perhaps this sense is not so common. Even if it were, it is not clear to the writer why common sense in a theory should be counted a defect.

Another objection levelled at Adler is that he attempts in his theory to moralize and to prescribe. He wrote a book entitled *What Life Should Mean to You* (1932). Science, so runs the objection, may say what life does mean to people, in the form of a large-scale survey, but it is the business of religion or ethics to say what it ought to mean. Value judgments are implicit in the title of Adler's book. He also writes in another place about the *correct* adaptation to the problems of work, love and community life. There are no scientific or objective criteria for moral correctness; Adler is going beyond the bounds of science. Undoubtedly he is. It is hard to see how he could be effective in helping humanity without prescribing remedies for its problems or guide-lines for it to live by. Few personality theorists, however scientific they may be, can remain totally neutral in a therapeutic situation. It was not Adler's intention to be neutral and non-directive and he must be judged accordingly. To measure his status by the yardstick of science may be inappropriate.

His is a subjective account of personality, that is to say, the personality is seen from within by the subject himself rather than from without by an observer. Adler attempts to understand the workings of personality by getting inside the other person as it were. Objective signs, such as mannerisms, appearance, etc., may provide clues, but all must be interpreted in the light of the individual's style of life. This subjective type of theory is the antithesis of Freud's. Freud studied the personality from without, that is to say, objectively; he minimized consciousness and emphasized biological causes. Adler made consciousness of central importance and stressed the individual's goals or guiding fictions. For Adler, man, since he creates himself, is much more the master of his fate than he is for Freud.

Conscious and unconscious are part of a unified personality in this theory. The unconscious is simply that part of consciousness which is not understood. It is no more than that which we have been unable to formulate in clear concepts. 'The conscious life becomes unconscious as soon as we fail to understand it, and as soon as we understand an unconscious tendency it has already become conscious' (1929). Freud believed repressed ideas deep in the unconscious had to be brought into consciousness to help recovery: Adler did not believe in repression; he saw a major part of the healer's task as being to help the patient to understand himself, to interpret and define his inner life. For Freud, repressed ideas were the main cause of the tension which caused neurotic breakdown: for Adler, the main cause was faulty adaptation to life. Helping him to understand himself might give the patient a clearer picture of his style of life and show him where this was at fault.

Some will argue that Adler makes man altogether too rational. Freud emphasized his irrationality and the importance of unconscious motives: Adler believed man is impelled by his rational strivings, drives being subordinated to these. Man is a nobler creature for Adler than for Freud. The two theories are strongly influenced by the very different views of man held by their creators. The Ansbachers (1956) suggest, using William James's distinction, that Adler was tender-minded (optimistic, idealistic, religious and feeling) whereas Freud was tough-minded (pessimistic, materialistic, irreligious and hardheaded). It is inconceivable that a psychologist's temperament and attitudes do not influence his theory of personality.

However this may be, does Adler in fact see man as being too rational? There is plenty of evidence of man's irrationality: widespread violence, two world wars, for example. Man hardly seems to be as socialized and rational

53

as Adler depicts him. And even if society be blamed for these disasters, it was individuals who created social systems and institutions. Man is ultimately responsible. That he is so rational is doubtful.

As well as ignoring man's non-rational nature, Adler has been accused of ignoring his biological drives. These are not in fact ignored: Adler admits, for instance, that sex is a powerful drive but not the dominant influence on personality. The striving for superiority supersedes all drives. The importance of biological factors in personality development is played down.

Whilst refusing to accept a determinist view of personality in which the instincts are prepotent, Adler refuses also to accept that the individual's personality is created solely by his social environment. A baby is born with certain predispositions or potentialities, for example that of social interest, but these are actualized by social influences. The theory is both social and psychological.

The idea of an innate potentiality for social interest seems to the writer as questionable as Freud's idea of innate anti-social tendencies. There is certainly less evidence of it in the overt behaviour of very young children. It seems to be an intrinsic element in Adler's optimistic view of human nature; his view of man predisposes him to believe in it.

Furthermore is it of any value to speak of a potentiality for social interest? Surely there are potentialities within an infant for all kinds of things, good or bad. Which of these is actualized depends very largely on environmental influences. An innate potentiality for social interest is just one of many innate potentialities. Adler would probably justify the attention he gives to this particular one by claiming that this is the one which most *needs* developing for the harmonious working of society.

It may also be claimed that Adler neglects the role of

learning in the development of personality. How does an individual learn to be a member of society? Adler certainly does not align himself with any school of learning theorists. He does, however, suggest that a young child may be socialized by withholding the reward of affection until the desired behaviour takes the place of the anti-social. He thus advocates the use by parents of a kind of operant conditioning. He also claims that influences of a social or educational kind are likely to be accepted only when they fit in with one's developing life-style, a fact which he believes constitutes an objection to a strictly behaviourist view. We learn what we see to be relevant to the attainment of our personal goal. The nature of the process by which things are learned is not discussed by Adler.

Not a great deal of research has been generated by Adler's theory of personality. However, birth order and the effect of the family constellation have received some attention. A number of characteristics have been found to be associated with being first-born in a family. The first child tends to have higher intelligence and to achieve more in life, but he also shows greater anxiety in stress situations and prefers to have company when in such a situation. He is more likely to seek psychotherapy than children from other family positions (Schachter, 1959; Altus, 1966). The successful research scientist is more likely than not to be a first son (Cattell and Brimhall, 1921). The only child, the fourth of Adler's well-defined types, was not found to be so clearly differentiated. Only very small differences were found in one study in which two matched groups of children with and without siblings were compared (Hooker, 1931).

It seems likely that early and intimate relationships within the family will exert an influence on attitudes for ever after. New relationships do to some extent duplicate old ones, and investigations have shown the kind of person

55

chosen as spouse or as a friend is determined partly by the kind of person lived with longest and most intimately. Thoman (1970) found that the most successful marriages were those between persons from complementary sibling positions in their own families: thus an older brother of sisters is more likely to make a happy marriage with a younger sister of brothers than with an older sister of brothers. A significantly greater number of divorces were found in marriages where there was full rank and sex conflict, for example, where an oldest brother of brothers married an oldest sister of sisters. The family constellation certainly contributes much to personality growth.

Although his theory as a whole has generated little research, there can be no doubt, as Brown (1961) suggests, that Adler has had a great influence on the thought of others, though this may often have been unconscious. Indeed, the Ansbachers (1956) demonstrate how in many of his ideas Adler anticipated Freud: for example, in 1908 Adler put forward the idea that a drive might be transformed into its opposite, an idea later taken over by Freud. Adler began by building on Freud's theory, but, because he seemed to be in a greater hurry, ended by anticipating Freud's own development. The Ansbachers question whether the so-called neo-Freudians might not be more fittingly named neo-Adlerians. Whilst their evidence for this seems convincing, the contention is still debatable. Of more importance for the teacher are Adler's views regarding education: to these we now turn.

Adler and education

Adler stands high among those psychologists who are concerned about the translation of theory into practical terms. He believed that Individual Psychology had an important contribution to make to social life. He was

56

greatly concerned with the psychology of early childhood and saw the role of motherhood as one of supreme importance: the mother taught the child the meaning of human fellowship and sought to extend his interest to embrace the welfare of society—to develop what Adler called social interest. Since there was no way of training all mothers to fulfil their maternal role, Adler believed he must teach the teachers the principles of human relationships and social interest. A large part of his time was given to presenting his views to teacher audiences and he even earned for himself the title of the greatest modern authority on education. His views have a decided relevance to modern educational thought and practice.

Adler saw the school as the prolonged arm of the family, an extension of the educational process going on in the home, and the teacher as counsellor, psychologist and friend. The teacher would stand *in loco parentis* and would have the task of noticing the difficulties of the children and correcting the mistakes made by the parents. A close partnership between home and school was essential for educational advancement. The teacher had a duty to correct a child's life-style where this was at fault and this might mean trying to eliminate damaging attitudes in the parents. Counselling sessions with parents were seen as part of the teacher-psychologist's job.

Individual Psychology does not offer any special teaching method or scheme, but it does suggest an attitude to the problems encountered. The problem of the unco-operative child is one example. It is the teacher's task to transform such a child from an antagonist into an ally, and this can never be achieved through punishment because that can never change a faulty attitude. The effect of punishment is to shame or humiliate the child, and no good educational results can come from that which harms a child's sense of prestige. Irony, used with general applica-

57

tion, might be permitted, but sarcasm addressed to the particular child should never be employed.

Adler was realist enough to grant that initially punishment, even corporal punishment, might be necessary, but one's aim as a teacher should be *gradually* to dispense with it. To have to rely on its excessive use, as the Plowden Report (1967) also affirms, is to acknowledge failure.

Many of the arguments heard in current debates about sex education in schools were used by Adler in his discussion of the subject. However, if to support sex teaching in schools is to align oneself with the 'progressives' in education, Adler would have had to relegate himself to the other camp. He did not see the classroom as the place for sex education. Teaching about sex was something which the child had to be ready to receive and this readiness was very much an individual matter; it could not be taught to a large class. Some children would already have been prepared to take a mistaken view if their parents' behaviour had taught them either to overvalue or undervalue sex. If the right attitude were present in the child even a 'street-corner explanation' would do him no harm. Adler would agree with Plowden (1967) that sex education is best given by parents in the context of a happy home, but, unlike Plowden, he appears to prefer the playground or street-corner explanation to the classroom one.

Adler asks two questions about how the class is to be regarded. They are as pertinent today as they were when he asked them. Is the class simply a place of instruction or has it an educational purpose beyond this? And second, is the class to be thought of as a corporate body or as a collection of individuals?

In answer to the first question, Adler believed the main purpose of the school was to teach the child how to live with his fellows—to socialize him. He wished to train each child to play his part harmoniously in the orchestra of society. This would be done by developing in him that social interest without which no child should be allowed to leave school. The social aims of education are regarded highly in our own time, the teacher's task being seen increasingly as one of transmitting values and attitudes rather than simply imparting information.

Adler's emphasis on the child as an individual led him to believe the teacher could not treat the class as a corporate body. Each child is unique and his own particular problems must be understood: no one can teach well if he does not know his pupils, insight into the child's psyche being essential for meeting his needs. Crowded classes are an obstacle to this kind of pupil-knowledge. Adler would be a strong supporter of the campaign for smaller classes. He also advocated the allocation of the same teacher to a class over three or four years; this would enable him effectively to remedy the mistakes in a pupil's style of life and to build the class into a co-operative social unit.

Adler's own social interest led him to be specially concerned for the weakling or the less successful child. Such a child needed to be helped to his feet rather than trampled underfoot. Therefore the use of competition in school was to be roundly decried; the co-operative spirit must always be encouraged. The more able must help the less able. Praise must take precedence over blame. Bad marks should never be given for fear of stopping a child from trying. Discouragement was the ultimate pedagogic sin and the backward class provided training in discouragement.

Adler would have welcomed the move towards de-streaming in the primary schools. Segregating children on the basis of their ability, he found, tended to divide children into those coming from richer and poorer homes. It discouraged the less able and deprived them of the stimulus brought to the class by its more intelligent members. In a competitive atmosphere, the bright children might deter;

in a co-operative one they would stimulate—a view shared by the Plowden Committee who believe the slower child is likely to gain from the enthusiasm and interests of his able neighbour.

There is a remarkably modern ring about Adler's views on the education of children. Individual Psychology seems to be enjoying something of a return to popularity in this country and perhaps the time will come when it will be given the place it deserves in the training of teachers. Spiel's account (1962) of his work at the Individual Psychology Experimental School should be read by all teachers who believe that education is more than simply imparting information.

5

Contrasting approaches: G. W. Allport and H. J. Eysenck

Biographical note

Gordon W. Allport was the second of four sons of a physician in the USA. He was born in 1897 in Indiana. His older brother, Floyd Allport, also became a psychologist of repute. G. W. Allport, after graduating at Harvard, taught and studied in various countries and became interested in international affairs. In 1930 he returned to Harvard as Professor of Psychology in the Department of Social Relations, and died in 1967.

Hans J. Eysenck was born in Germany but came to England because of Nazism in 1934 and received his Ph.D. in Psychology at London University. He is now both Professor of Psychology in the University of London and Director of the Psychological Department at the Institute of Psychiatry. He thus combines academic, experimental and clinical work. In addition to his work in the field of personality, he has recently investigated the application of principles of learning to the treatment of the neuroses (1965a).

Differing standpoints

The reason for considering these two psychologists together must be made clear at the outset. They are representative of two different approaches to the study of personality. They agree on some aspects (their definitions are similar), they have certain concepts in common but they start from different theoretical positions and, by and large, use different methods. They differ in their ideas about the nature of personality study and the precise phenomena to which their attention should be given.

The term 'personality' may be used, as Allport (1963) points out, to refer both to man in particular and to man in general. Thus we may say of someone we know that he has a very interesting personality; on the other hand, we may refer to personality as an interesting phenomenon. A moment's reflection will make it clear that we use the word in these two ways quite often. The important question is: which is the relevant meaning for the psychology of personality? Allport and Eysenck answer in different ways: Allport considers that our attention should primarily be directed to individuality (man-in-particular); Eysenck believes man-in-general is the only legitimate object of scientific study in this field. Allport's approach has been called *idiographic*, concerned with the specific behaviour of an individual; Eysenck's is *nomothetic*, concerned with formulating laws about people in general. Allport suggests that *morphogenic* is preferable to describe his approach and *dimensional* the other approach. What are the reasons behind their favouring these different standpoints?

The conflict has a lengthy historical background. The medieval schoolmen maintained that science was not concerned with individuals, and, despite its obvious falseness (see Holt, 1962), the idea dies hard. There is still the belief that science is defined by its subject-matter rather than

62

by its method. To contend that universals and general laws are the only legitimate concern of science is to exclude the possibility of the scientific study of the individual.

Those who believe that the psychology of personality is nomothetic are eager to discover general laws which will enable us to predict the behaviour of all individuals. They believe in scientific explanation based on objective evidence, and they make use of precise methods such as standardized questionnaires, physiological measures and situational tests. From the idiographic standpoint, their work is sterile and irrelevant, since, although it may measure elements of behaviour (traits of personality), it ignores the question of how these traits inter-relate to form the unique individual. It produces what Allport has described as an uncemented mosaic of elements (1963). The idiographic theorists are interested in how the pieces are cemented together in an individual case, no two individuals being alike. To discover this they favour an understanding approach as opposed to an explanatory one. They make use of personal documents (letters, diaries), open-ended questions, case-histories and autobiographies; the subject's own self-knowledge is an important source of data. Their approach involves empathic feeling, seeking to know the individual from within by non-intellective means—in short, understanding him rather than explaining him. Allport believes that too much personality study has been concerned with 'commonalities' amongst human beings, and his aim is to redress this one-sidedness by urging a morphogenic approach.

Eysenck does not agree. Science is concerned with quantifying and the psychology of personality must use the methods of science. The scientific approach emphasizes the ways in which men are alike. A nomothetic science makes large-scale investigations comprising thousands of individuals and producing general laws; studying the individual has value only as a source for hypotheses, not as science. Although Allport believes that the generalizations arrived at by the nomothetic approach are not meaningful since they do not apply to anyone at all, Eysenck replies that they are the most meaningful statements about personality that have any value in science.

Are these two approaches irreconcilable in the study of personality? Holt (1962) claims that neither the nomothetic nor the idiographic method of studying personality is satisfactory: the former is a caricature of science, springing in part from the false premise that science is defined by its subject-matter rather than its method; the latter seeks an artistic goal which is more properly the aim of the literary biographer. Holt believes both terms should be dropped from the study of personality.

However, what of the two approaches signified by these terms? May they not both have something to offer? Intuition and empathy are inevitable components, in some degree, of any hypothesis formed by a human being in whatever field he is working. They may and must be excluded, however, from the assessment of the predictive value of the hypothesis—from the testing phase: here objectivity must prevail. Allport aims at understanding: Eysenck at prediction and control. As Holt points out, all highly developed sciences aim at control through understanding. (The medieval schoolmen sought to understand nature so as to dominate it.) Perhaps the two psychologists we are considering are emphasizing different parts of a total process. Neither, after all, ignores what is of prior importance to the other: Eysenck admits the study of the individual helps in forming hypotheses; Allport accepts that generalizations, albeit only approximations, do have their uses. We turn now to a brief consideration of their distinctive contributions to the psychology of personality.

Allport's theory

Allport, whilst not entirely happy with any definition of personality, settles for this: 'personality is the dynamic organization within the individual of those psychophysical systems that determine his characteristic behaviour and thought' (Allport, 1963). The words used are full of meaning: it is a *dynamic organization*—its elements are patterned or organized in a unique way and this patterning directs the individual's activity; it is *psychophysical*—mind and body function together to produce an individual personality; behaviour and thought are *characteristic* in that a particular pattern applies to one person and to no other —every individual is unique.

Traits seem to Allport to be the most acceptable unit of investigation in personality study (1937). They are not directly observable but are inferred from behaviour: thus, if a person regularly cheats the taxman, steals from his employer and tells lies, we may deduce the trait of dishonesty. But there are dangers with traits. Behaviour is a continuous flow, and traits are not like 'little men in the breast', each responsible for a separate type of activity. No trait determines behaviour all by itself. Nor are traits consistently found within an individual: a man may be dishonest in many situations but strictly honest in others.

Traits may be divided into common traits and individual traits. The latter Allport prefers to call personal dispositions. Common traits denote the aspects of personality in relation to which comparison between the different members of a particular culture is possible. They are artefacts, that is to say they do not correspond exactly to the characteristics of any person in reality; they are approximations, and to describe an individual in terms of common traits is to violate his real personality because it means ignoring the actual system operating uniquely within him.

Common traits are discovered by standardized questionnaires and similar tests. Their discovery may be useful in that they indicate the areas where important personal dispositions may be found by careful further investigation. When these are found, the individual's personality structure is accurately reflected; they reveal his particular internal patterning. The resulting picture corresponds to something that exists in the real world.

Personal dispositions are able to initiate and guide behaviour. They are thus part of a person's motivational system. Indeed they may be the leading motives in his life, determining the way he meets his environment. Allport does not accept the idea that unconscious motives are important; the dominant motivation is at the conscious level. Further, the motives behind the same activity are constantly changing. Psychoanalytic theory is wrong in always digging into an individual's past to understand his behaviour. He can best be understood in relation to what he is striving for in the future. His intentions are the most important key to his present behaviour. (Notice here the strong similarity to Adler's motivational viewpoint.)

The best known and most controversial of Allport's concepts is the *functional autonomy* of motives. By this he means that any activity may become an end in itself, totally detached from the motives out of which it originated. Motives are contemporary; they are not bound to their historical origins. A hunter may begin to hunt because he needs food; he may hunt in later life simply because he likes doing so. His present behaviour is independent of the needs which originally produced it. Allport cites (1971), as an example of functionally autonomous behaviour, the phenomenon of the son following the father's profession: in US politics, for example, the Kennedys, Tafts and Roosevelts may have imitated their fathers at six because of the father identification common

66

at that age, but it would be absurd to assume that their work in the Senate forty years later still represented an attempt to be daddy. The character of motives alters radically from childhood to adulthood and the extent to which adult motives replace childish ones is an indication of a person's level of maturity.

The growth towards maturity is intimately linked with the notion of the functional autonomy of motives. The new-born infant is largely a creature of heredity, possessing reflexes and being dominated by basic drives such as hunger. Temperament, the 'chemical climate' or emotional nature, is there, but no personality. Tensions exist and initiate motivation which is aimed at removing these and promoting pleasure, but, as self-awareness develops, this tension-reducing model becomes less acceptable; conscious motives, linked with such phenomena as identification and the self-image, become important. What was mechanical becomes autonomous or self-directing. The highly individualized traits that have developed out of the interaction of temperament (internal weather) and environment (external weather) motivate the person in ways that are largely conscious and rational.

However, some adults still seem to be motivated by infantile drives. Their behaviour is more closely linked to the childhood state than to their adult aspirations and goals. They do not know why they act as they do; they are seriously disturbed. By contrast, the mature adult knows what motivates him.

Maturity is marked by certain characteristics: the mature personality shows an *extension of the self*, that is, he has strong interests which are quite outside himself, completely unrelated to his own creature-comforts. His interests are not egocentric or determined by his bodily needs: they extend to the spheres of recreation, education, politics, religion, to mention but a few. Second, the mature

67

personality has the *capacity to view himself objectively*: he has insight into himself (measurable by the degree of correspondence between what he thinks he is and what most others think he is), and he can laugh at himself whilst still accepting himself. Third, the mature personality has *a unifying philosophy of life*, a set of convictions—religious, aesthetic, political or of some other kind—which gives meaning and purpose to his behaviour and direction to his life. These criteria for maturity are drawn by Allport from a survey of some of the vast literature on what normality, health and maturity mean in western culture.

Allport's theory of personality has little in it that is original: he has said that he believes it is better to be both eclectic and tentative. His two major conclusions, or emphases, are (1) that the individual is divorced from his past and (2) that he is unique. The first arises from the fact that his motives are functionally autonomous; the second means that perhaps psychology can never measure him adequately. As a theory, Allport's account of personality is poor: how the assumptions are inter-related is not clear, and some of the concepts, for example functional autonomy, do not seem to lend themselves to empirical translation. Neither does it satisfy the other criterion referred to in chapter 2: it has led to very little investigation and research; it is of low predictive value. Nevertheless, it contains some interesting ideas and does clarify certain commonly used terms. In its morphogenic emphasis, it is a useful reminder of the possible limitations of a scientific approach to personality. American clinical psychologists have found Allport's writing of value in their day-to-day work, declaring his influence to be second only to that of Freud (Schafer *et al.*, 1951).

Eysenck's theory

Eysenck (1960) defines personality in a way which, he admits, owes much to Allport, as 'the more or less stable and enduring organization of a person's character, temperament, intellect and physique which determine his unique adjustment to the environment'. Elsewhere he has defined it as the sum total of the behaviour patterns of the organism. Like the scientist he is, he is more interested in how a characteristic of one individual compares with the same characteristic of men in general than in how that characteristic links with the other characteristics within the individual. What is common to mankind he believes to be of more value in science than what is specific to one individual. As we shall see, for Eysenck, the individual is a point of intersection plotted on a number of quantitative variables. This is what for the scientist Eysenck believes he must be.

How is personality to be described? Eysenck finds the concepts of trait and type both relevant for this purpose. We arrive at a trait by observing constancies in his behaviour: thus the man to whom the trait persistence applies is one who in a variety of specific situations always responds in the same dogged way, being neither distracted by other activities nor put off by boredom or fatigue. A trait is deduced from behaviour in a large number of different situations. Tests may be devised by the experimenter to measure the degree to which the trait is shown in different situations (for example, see Eysenck, 1957, chapter 5). Traits, then, are made up from habitual responses by the individual. Type is a more inclusive concept: it refers to a group of traits which are correlated with one another, that is to say, found grouped together again and again. The *introvert* type, for example, always embraces traits such as shyness, persistence, rigidity and

69

so on. The type is the highest level of behaviour organization.

Eysenck's theory stresses the importance of heredity. Personality is considerably determined by genetic endowment. The innate reactivity of the autonomic nervous system underlies an individual's emotionality, and the neurological functioning of his brain, particularly of a hitherto little understood part of the brain stem, known as the ascending reticular formation, underlies the degree to which he is extraverted or introverted. By considering an individual's position on the two dimensions of emotionality or neuroticism (stability-instability) and of extraversion-introversion, and taking into account his level of intelligence, we know just about as much as can be known scientifically about his personality.

How did Eysenck reach this conclusion? His discovery of the major dimensions of personality resulted from large-scale investigations involving thousands of subjects. Using a statistical technique known as *factor analysis*, formerly used by Spearman in connection with intellectual processes, Eysenck discovered those traits which characterized neurotics in such a way as to distinguish them from normal people. Briefly, the technique involves applying a battery of tests of various kinds so as to collect a lot of data about behaviour, then finding out what underlying factors are responsible for the variations in behaviour by correlating the results of the tests, and finally trying to devise more efficient measures of the factors discovered.

As a result of his original investigation, Eysenck established the dimension of neuroticism. Imagine this as a line or a continuum with the very stable, non-emotional individuals at one end and the highly unstable individuals at the other. The person high in neuroticism will show some of the following traits: moodiness, restlessness, high anxiety, touchiness, aggressiveness. At the other end of the continuum will be the calm, even-tempered, carefree and thoroughly reliable individuals. Most people will have intermediate positions on the dimension. Eysenck continued his investigation by testing those on the unstable half of the dimension. He found that those people who were relatively high in neuroticism still did not form a homogeneous group. They differed from one another in that the members of one group were characterized by excessive tiredness, constant introspection, feelings of guilt and an over-concern with religious and ethical matters, whilst the other group were impulsive, changeable, irresponsible and lacking in moral fibre. The first Eysenck called the *dysthymic* group; the second, the *hysteric*. The next stage was to see if those on the stable half of the dimension differed from one another in corresponding ways. The application of factor analysis showed that they did. This meant there were therefore two independent dimensions along which people differed from one another. Since the dysthymics resembled the *introvert* as described by Jung (1923) and the hysterics the *extravert*, Eysenck adopted these terms for the second dimension. Again it is important to point out, as Jung originally did, that no person is totally extraverted or totally introverted; it is the relative strength of the psychic functions in relation to each other which determines the personality. The pure type does not exist in reality, and the person who seems to be extremely introverted may yet in an exceptional case show extraverted behaviour.

Bearing this always in mind, let us consider the characteristics of extraverts and introverts, since Eysenck's two major dimensions will provide the theoretical background for our consideration of the personality attributes likely to make for success in learning and teaching (chapters 6 and 7). The extreme extravert values the outer world much more than his own inner world of ideas; his energies are directed outwards. He is active and sociable, always seeking excitement, enjoying change, acting on impulse. He does not like reading or studying by himself. He likes practical jokes and 'enjoys a good laugh'. He loses his temper quickly but is unlikely to harbour a grudge for long; his feelings, unlike still waters, do not run deep. It is the introvert who is more impassioned in the sense that, though they are less easily roused, his feelings are much more enduring. He does not lose his temper easily but builds up strong dislikes over a long period; on the other hand, his attachments to others are deeper and he is the more constant friend. The introvert is more introspective, needs less stimulation from the external world, is less ambitious and less interested in material things. He plans ahead and likes an ordered life. He is more serious-minded and less aggressive.

According to Eysenck (1965b), the introvert shows this pattern of behaviour because of the functioning of the ascending reticular formation in the brain stem. The latter either excites or inhibits the activity of the cortex in dealing with incoming sensory impulses. Where the level of stimulation getting through to the cortex is depressed or inhibited, the individual will be driven to seek more stimulation from the external world: his behaviour will be extraverted. Conversely, where the incoming stimulation is amplified, over-bombardment of the cortex will lead to introverted behaviour patterns. This description is both brief and crude, but the explanation is useful and there is much evidence to suggest that it is along the right lines.

Eysenck's theory attempts to classify human behaviour rather than to understand the individual. This is in keeping with his belief that measurement is essential for scientific advance, and that the classification of behaviour is the vital first step for carrying out that measurement. The theory has many applications, for example, in our understanding of the delinquent, the criminal and the offending motorist (1964). Eysenck is also concerned with methods of curing phobias and other neurotic manifestations by the use of behaviour therapy, a technique derived directly from classical conditioning. His researches have greatly increased our understanding of man in general, and his findings form a useful basis for prediction in various spheres.

6

Personality and learning

Introductory

This chapter, and the one that follows it, could be said to represent the core of the book. We are concerned here to discover what aspects of personality are positively related to success in learning. Our concern arises from the conviction that intellectual ability, though a necessary condition for success in learning, is not a sufficient condition. The prediction and understanding of achievement in the learning sphere demands that we pay attention to both personality traits and motivation. Cattell *et al.* (1966) maintain that personality and motivation account for much of the variance in pupils' achievement, and that the predictive power of tests used in schools would be increased by the inclusion of personality and motivation measures. Achievement seems to be the result of the interaction of intelligence, personality and motivation.

One of our major problems is how to measure success. Exactly when may a pupil be described as successful? In our culture success is usually assessed in relation to examinations passed and level of qualifications acquired. This, together with teachers' ratings and standardized attainment test scores, is the criterion used in most of the studies to which reference is made.

74

Much of the recent work on personality characteristics in relation to pupil achievement has been based on Eysenck's dimensions of neuroticism and extraversion-introversion discussed in the previous chapter. Where the studies have been based on other personality variables attempts will be made to suggest links with Eysenck's dimensions. Some of the writer's speculation has been allowed to creep in and may possibly either provoke discussion or suggest lines for future research. This at least is his hope.

Extraversion–introversion and learning

There are two quite distinct types of learning and it will be as well to differentiate between them at the outset. The first type refers to what goes on in school when an individual stores up information and develops a system of knowledge as, for example, in learning geography. The second is more general: it refers to the changes in our behaviour in response to events that have an effect on us, to the new responses that are developed to new and familiar stimuli. Conditioning is the major factor in this type of learning. Conscious memorizing is not part of it.

This distinction is pointed out because without it one might assume that the evidence showing that introverts are more readily conditioned than extraverts in an experimental situation indicated that introverts would learn school subjects more quickly than extraverts. Such an assumption is not warranted by this evidence.

The findings are in fact rather complex and show the need to consider this dimension of personality in relation to the age and sex of the subject studied. Some of the evidence is in conflict unless these variables are taken into consideration. By and large, the findings of different investigators concur fairly well.

Beginning with research on primary school children, a study of ninety-three children around the age of eight years by Savage (1966) revealed that children high in extraversion, this being determined by their score on the Eysenck Personality Inventory (EPI), had higher academic attainment scores than the others. This link between extraversion and attainment at the junior level receives further support from a study of 458 eleven-year-olds by Rushton (1966). He used the Cattell Children's Personality Questionnaire and investigated the relationship between personality so assessed and four Moray House cognitive ability measures. His conclusion was that extraversion is positively correlated with academic success at eleven. A third piece of evidence comes from a large-scale investigation by Eysenck and Cookson (1969) using 4,000 eleven-year-olds. They were given the Junior EPI and the results were analysed in relation to performance on two Moray House tests (maths and English) and the Schonell Graded Word-Reading Test. The scholastic superiority of extraverted boys and girls was revealed yet again, and stable extraverted children were the most favoured group in respect of entrance to selective grammar schools in the region.

As we move into secondary education, a different picture begins to emerge. Ridding (1967) used 600 pupils aged twelve plus and found that the extraverts were still doing better, in that their attainment scores were higher than their scores on a Moray House verbal reasoning test would lead one to expect—they were over-achieving. Introverts, on the other hand, were under-achieving. Entwistle and Cunningham (1968), however, using nearly 3,000 children of around thirteen years, found no significant correlation between extraversion and attainment. Their finding was very interesting. It emerged that girls who were extraverted and boys who were introverted, measured on the JEPI, did better than introverted girls and extraverted boys.

Any explanation of this finding can only be speculative. It may be that peer group values for the thirteen-year-old boy are away from academic success, so that the extravert boy who is more strongly influenced by his peer group stops trying hard in school. Perhaps girls' peer group values at this age support academic prowess, but it is still hard to see why the female introvert lags behind despite her more studious nature. A later study by Entwistle and Welsh (1969), using 2,538 children between eleven and fourteen years, found extraversion to be negatively related with attainment among bright boys and to a lesser extent among bright girls, but among the less able of both sexes, extraversion and attainment were positively related. Ability therefore was a relevant variable: introverts of high ability and extraverts of lower ability were the best achievers.

It looks as if the majority of entrants to the universities have a tendency to be introverted. There is evidence that, in Britain anyway, the university population is more introverted than the population at large. A study by Lynn and Gordon (1961), using sixty male university students aged eighteen to twenty-three years, found a relationship between introversion and academic success. Since there is no significant correlation between introversion and level of intelligence, they proposed that the relationship must be in connection with the introvert's ability to apply himself to his work. Introverts tire less quickly than extraverts, probably because of the neurological differences referred to at the end of the last chapter. There is, moreover, a significant level of proof for a positive correlation between introversion and persistence. Numerous studies have shown that university students tend to excel when high on introversion. This may well be because, as the Entwistles (1970) found, introverts have better study methods than extraverts. Kline (1966) found that introversion was strongly related to academic success in Ghanaian university

77

students, indicating that even in a culture pattern very different from that in Britain, this personality factor had a similar influence. However, Kline and Gale (1971), using Exeter University students, found no stable correlation between success in a university examination and either introversion or extraversion. They therefore urge caution in stating, as a general finding, that academic success is positively related to introversion, though the majority of studies do suggest this.

The evidence indicates, then, that whilst extraverts do better at the junior school level, it is the introverts who obtain the best university degrees. Selection at eleven plus favours the extraverts but these are ultimately overtaken by the introverts. Do the children who are extraverted at eleven become introverted by the time they are eighteen? This is highly improbable if we accept that extraversion–introversion has a neurological basis. Is the change to be explained in terms of the different conditions for success at eleven and eighteen? To be successful at eleven, persistence and long spells of concentrated work are not essential; at eighteen, they are. Junior school activities are very different from sixth-form ones. So-called progressive methods appeal to extraverts whilst the traditional academic approach fits the introvert better.

That particular teaching strategies may be more effective with one type of personality than with another is suggested by the results of a study by Trown (1970). Using as subjects 250 eleven- and twelve-year-olds of all ability levels, she found a persistent suggestion that when in mathematics rules were presented before examples, introverts were superior in performance, whereas when rules were given after examples, the extraverts were superior. No categorical statement should be made on the basis of this suggestion, as Trown points out, but it points the way for future research. Can teaching strategy and personality be matched to give optimal results? Is programmed learning, for example, more effective with one type of personality than with another?

Another interesting line of investigation concerns the relation of speed of working and personality type. Using problems of the type found in intelligence tests, Farley (1966) found that extraverts were significantly faster than both introverts and ambiverts (those about the mid-point on the continuum) at solving the problems correctly. Eysenck (1959) had found that extraverts were quicker in a sixty-problem test on the first forty-five questions but slower on the last fifteen, suggesting that once the introvert got 'into the swing' of solving the problems his speed increased, whilst the extravert, after a quick start, slowed down (presumably as reactive inhibition built up), and, as was also shown, gave in sooner in the face of difficulty. It looks rather like the hare and the tortoise story all over again! It lends support to the idea that the introvert, slower initially but ultimately the more successful, may be the type commonly referred to as the 'late developer'.

It would be interesting to discover whether successful extraverts and introverts are attracted by different subject-disciplines, rather like the convergers and divergers described by Hudson (1966). Eysenck and Cookson (1969) suggest tentatively that introverts may be predisposed towards scientific achievement and extraverts towards linguistic attainment. Hudson found that convergers were more scientifically oriented and divergers tended towards arts subjects. This might suggest a link between introversion and convergent thinking and extraversion and divergent thinking. Such a link seems to concur with common experience. However, Hudson (1968) found a near to zero relationship between introversion and convergent thinking and suggests that the cognitive styles he studied are not related to this personality factor.

Stability and learning

We turn our attention now to the neuroticism dimension discovered by Eysenck to see what relevance it has to successful learning. In some ways it seems more likely to be relevant because everyone is familiar with something called an 'emotional block' and we all know that when our emotions are roused learning becomes more difficult. People obviously vary in their emotionality or neuroticism. Those high on this factor are likely to show anxiety and indecision, to be unable to concentrate and to have irrational fears. It has also been found that they lack perseverance in the face of obstacles and are likely to give in or break down easily. Anxiety seems to be a major component of neuroticism and a good many studies have been directed towards anxiety. It seems to be worthy of attention because of its relation to drive and level of motivation.

High anxiety comprises dread and strong apprehension, but this shades off into slight feelings of uneasiness such as might be produced in children presented with an unsolved problem. What happens in this situation is that the psychological equilibrium is upset and there is an increase in alertness and drive aimed at restoring equilibrium. This anxiety is mild and is highly specific in its aim; it facilitates action rather than disrupts it. Children to whom this kind of anxiety is natural are likely to be more strongly motivated than average. We might therefore be justified in expecting such children to do well in contrast with those whose anxiety is general and strong enough to be disruptive.

Tests have been devised to measure the anxiety level of the individual. Research workers have also shown that whether or not anxiety helps to promote better attainment depends considerably on the task being performed. When

80

the work is very complex, the child high in anxiety does less well than others, but on simple tasks the highly anxious child does better. Anxiety to succeed will make for superior attainment except where the task is very complex and the level of anxiety so high as to be disruptive.

Empirical studies of the relation of anxiety or neuroticism to attainment have produced some conflicting results. Here, as with extraversion–introversion, it is necessary to take into account the age of the subjects. At the junior level, Savage (1966) found that the correlation between neuroticism and academic success was not significant in eight-year-olds, and Rushton (1966), working with eleven-year-olds, found that anxiety had a negative correlation with verbal reasoning, English, arithmetic and teacher's rating. It would seem that the less anxious child is the more successful at this stage and that low neuroticism makes for better attainment. Astington (1960) had likewise discovered that the most successful primary school boys were more emotionally stable than the less successful ones. However, the large-scale study by Eysenck and Cookson (1969) indicated that stable boys and girls did only marginally better than unstable ones. Introversion–extraversion scores seemed to be more reliable as predictors of scholastic success.

The superiority of stable pupils seems to hold true at the secondary level also, though the evidence is suggestive rather than conclusive. Astington (1960) found that, as at the primary stage, the most successful boys were more emotionally stable, but he also found they were slightly more nervous than the less successful ones. Perhaps this means they had rather more of that specific task-anxiety discussed earlier and this motivated them to do well. Certainly the general anxiety associated with neuroticism was found by Child (1964) to be negatively correlated with achievement in the comprehensive school pupils he used.

Entwistle and Cunningham (1968) found a similar negative relation between neuroticism and attainment in the 2,700 thirteen-year-olds they studied. Stable children showed the highest attainment scores. On the other hand, Ridding (1967), using a smaller sample of twelve-year-olds, found that stability and anxiety were equally irrelevant to over- or under-achievement.

If stability seems to be the most likely predictor of success at the junior and secondary level, what is the state of things at the tertiary level? The Eysencks (1969) claim that it is the neurotic introvert who is the most successful student. This had first been proposed by Furneaux (1962) who further pointed out that 60 per cent of stable extraverts fail their university examinations. Lynn and Gordon (1961) suggest that the optimal level of neuroticism for academic performance seemed to be about half a standard deviation above the national average. They noted an interesting positive relation between neuroticism and size of vocabulary; it is just possible this might have a bearing on success in essay-type examinations. In general, however, emotional instability or neuroticism has a less certain relation to academic success than introversion at this level. American studies seem to suggest the superiority of *stable* introverts, and Entwistle and Wilson (1970) found no link between neuroticism and degree class, though introverts gained more good honours degrees. These findings were based on Aberdeen students: at Lancaster, the Entwistles (1970) also found no relationship between neuroticism and academic attainment. They used both university and college of education students in this study. They found that the stable introvert was on the whole the most successful and had good work habits, whilst the unstable introvert tended to have a higher level of motivation and to work longer hours. If the unstable student can allay the nagging worries that assail him, his higher than average motivation may spur him to success. The stable extravert probably enjoys his social life too much and has a 'couldn't-care-less' attitude to his work. The most recent evidence certainly supports the idea, which common sense would surely favour too, that the stable introvert is the most successful student.

7

Personality and teaching

Introductory

The evidence on the relation of personality variables to achievement in school, whilst not conclusive, is at least strongly suggestive. This is more than can be said for much of the evidence on the relation of personality variables to success in teaching. There is a good deal of contradiction here, particularly in relation to Eysenck's extraversion–introversion dimension. A large part of the difficulty undoubtedly lies in the highly complex nature of the criterion embodied in the term teacher effectiveness.

What does it mean to be an effective teacher? First of all the term teacher is so broad in its denotation: it may be applied equally to a university lecturer or tutor and to the teacher of a reception class in a primary school. A very wide range of activities is implied, from resolving abstruse philosophical problems to helping a child feel secure on his first day at school. Quite obviously the same person may be very good at one of these tasks and totally incompetent at the other, though it is quite possible for someone to be good at both. Some recognition of the diverseness of the teacher's role is implied by the request of the James Committee (1972) to make the professional training of the teacher 'unashamedly specialized and functional'. The term teacher may mean so many different things.

Much more so the term effective. For our purposes, effective and successful may be thought of as synonymous, but we still need to know what the criterion for effectiveness or success might be. Pupil achievement (i.e. number of examination passes) has been considered a criterion and it has at least the advantage of being exactly measurable. Surely, however, there is more to good teaching than pushing pupils through examinations—this would be a very narrow conception, though of course pupil achievement must be a part of the end-product of good teaching.

Being liked by one's pupils may well be a mark of an effective teacher though we must avoid the assumption that to be popular and to be respected are one and the same. Taylor (1962) found that both primary and secondary school pupils believed the good teacher to be cheerful, good-tempered, patient, understanding, kind, sympathetic and to have a sense of humour. The judgments of the pupils are of considerable importance but there is more to teacher effectiveness than being liked by one's pupils. One may be popular without making any significant contributions to one's pupils' intellectual development.

A more complete measure of effectiveness is a rating by head-teachers, inspectors or other qualified assessors, but here again there are serious difficulties. The rating presupposes criteria, and these cannot escape the charge of subjectivity. The grade given is likely to reflect the degree of similarities between the educational 'philosophies' of the rater and the ratee, or the degree of rapport between their personalities. It requires a superman to award a distinction grade to a teacher he detests!

A less-than-desirable agreement has been found between ratings by college assessors during training and later assessments of effectiveness. Much obviously depends on how far the student is in sympathy with the kind of school he is in and the kind of child he is teaching, but there is also some indication that, in Australia anyway, 'attractive' girls receive higher grades than others when rated by male senior teachers! (Hore, 1971.)

The problems linked with finding an acceptable criterion for teacher effectiveness are legion. The role of the teacher is so diverse and the criteria of effectiveness so subjective that it is hard to know where to start. The evidence so far suggests that there is no one pattern of successful teacher, and it is true, as Getzels and Jackson (1963) have said, that very little is known for certain about the relation between teacher personality and teaching effectiveness, but, amidst the diversity, two prerequisites of teaching success seem to stand out. The first is intelligence, i.e. the power to discern and utilize relationships, without which good teaching would be impossible. Above a certain minimum level, however, I.Q. has no measurable effect upon teaching ability (Crocker, 1968). The second, if it be true, as frequently stated, that teaching implies first and foremost human interaction, is a capacity for making good human relationships.

Extraversion–introversion and teaching

One of the earliest investigations in the field of teacher effectiveness was that of Birkinshaw (1935). She used as subjects over 3,000 women teachers working in rural and urban areas throughout England. These were teachers of all ages and it is interesting to note that only seven out of this large sample were married—an indication of how times have changed. One of the main conclusions of this research was that the extraverted person was the more successful teacher because an extravert likes to share the interests of other people and to share her own interests with them, and doing this was a necessary part of teaching. The introvert, on the other hand, with her natural tendency to turn inwards away from contact with the world was unlikely to succeed as a teacher.

Birkinshaw's survey was, of course, carried out several years before Eysenck discovered the trait dimension to which he gave the name extraversion–introversion and devised his personality inventories. It was also carried out many years before Cattell, in the USA, devised his Sixteen Personality Factor Questionnaire, a test widely used in attempts to relate personality characteristics to teaching effectiveness. More work in this connection seems to have been based on the latter test than on Eysenck's tests, possibly because more work has been done in America than in Britain. An important difference between the tests lies in the fact that, whereas Eysenck regards extraversion and introversion as unitary traits, Cattell, also using factor analysis, holds that these terms refer to clusters of traits all intercorrelating positively and significantly. Extraversion, for Cattell (1965), is a 'surface trait', observed superficially but underlaid by a number of unitary 'source traits'. In studies based on Cattell's work we have to consider the relation of the source traits found to be correlated with teaching success to the wider concepts of extraversion and introversion.

A study descriptive of trainee teachers rather than prescriptive of teacher effectiveness was made by A. J. Singh (1969). Using the Maudesley Personality Inventory (MPI), devised by Eysenck, he found that, in his sample of 302 students, those who were specializing in education had the highest mean score in extraversion compared with students specializing in humanities, science or social science. Perhaps we may deduce from this that teaching attracts extraverts. Another study, by Soloman (1965), using the MPI and other tests with mature training college students, indicated a connection between extravert qualities and success in the training course. A major conclusion of Soloman's research was that the successful teacher was a woman with a certain tenseness of personality which produced a 'live-wire' quality in the classroom and made her alert to children's needs. She was fluent and lively, warm, sociable and cheerful. It would be useful if more attempts were made to correlate scores on the MPI with level of teaching ability.

Cattell's 16 PF Inventory has been used on both sides of the Atlantic but the results are very inconclusive. Lamke (1951), using ten teachers rated as good and eight rated poor, found the good teachers to be more talkative, cheerful, placid, content, open and quicker than average, that is, they ranked high on source trait F which was separated out from the surface trait of extraversion–introversion. The poor teachers were lower than average on this trait, which also measures such qualities as resourcefulness, humour, sociability and responsiveness. The good teachers were also above average on source trait H: they were more gregarious, adventurous and frivolous, had stronger artistic or sentimental interests and were more interested in the opposite sex. According to Cattell, the qualities associated with F have a strong connection with the individual's background and upbringing whereas those associated with H are strongly linked with heredity. It is also interesting to note Cattell's finding that F is high in salesmen, executives and professional athletes but low in engineers, nurses and electricians. Teachers should therefore have more in common with the former than the latter! Unfortunately for our purposes, Cattell does not find that F correlates highly with extraversion, though superficially it does seem to resemble that trait.

Again unfortunately for those seeking a clear-cut answer,

some British research by Start (1966) comes to the conclusion that better teachers are *not* warmer and more sociable than the average teacher. The rating of teacher competence in the secondary modern school involved in this study was by the head-teacher. The 16 PF test showed the best teachers were significantly higher on general intelligence, dominance, relaxed security, conservatism, introversion and individuality. They are less concerned with striving to conform to socially approved behaviour patterns, and it is the average and below average teachers who tend to be the most sociable.

How do we explain the apparent contradiction in the findings of Lamke and Start? The same test was used but it is hard to say whether this is the case with the criteria of effectiveness. Start's teachers were rated by one individual; Lamke's by three. The studies were in different parts of the world; the teachers were working in what doubtless were very different situations. It is interesting and worth while to note that some studies have failed to find any significant correlations between 16 PF scores and teaching ability (e.g. Cortis, 1968).

In their attitudes, Eysenck has found extraverts to be more tough-minded and introverts more tender-minded. That is to say, the introvert is more likely to be against capital punishment, racial discrimination, the flogging of criminals and other such practices. He is more idealistic and has a keener religious and ethical sense. In view of this link between introversion and tender-mindedness, the study by Warburton *et al.* (1963) seems to suggest that the good teacher has more in common with the introvert. The most successful student-teachers had tender-minded educational attitudes. On the 16 PF test they scored high on source trait I which suggests a high degree of sensitive imagination and aesthetic fastidiousness. This trait has a low correlation with popularity probably because of its

89

associated unwillingness to be realistic, yet students high on this trait were awarded better final teaching marks. Cattell also found teachers significantly above average on this trait, in common with housewives, hairdressers and waitresses among others, and in contrast to airline pilots, electricians and priests! On the other hand, lest we should think we are getting somewhere, Davis and Satterly (1969), working with students from Homerton College of Education, found that a high score on factor I correlated with poor teaching. Higher than average sensitivity, they found, militated against a high teaching grade.

Yet another set of contradicting results come from studies by Schmid (1950) and Singer (1954). Using a well-known test, the Minnesota Multiphasic Personality Inventory (MMPI), Schmid, using female subjects only, found that introversive behaviour was linked with low teaching ability. Singer, on the other hand, using the same test but with subjects of both sexes, found a positive correlation between social introversion and overall teaching effectiveness.

In the absence of more conclusive evidence relating to extraversion–introversion and teaching ability, one can only speculate and continue to investigate possible connections. It would surely be reasonable to expect that, in a job essentially concerned with relations with other people, extraverts would be more successful, at least initially. Perhaps the introvert may be a slow starter and may prove his worth after a period of time; his typically greater conscientiousness may be expected to help.

One might reasonably expect also that the extravert would be more effective in teaching where relationships are the major consideration whilst the introvert would succeed where the subject-matter is more important. Thus, putting it simply, extraverts should make better primary and middle school teachers and introverts better sixth-form and university teachers. Certainly the level at which the teaching is being carried out is a very relevant variable not sufficiently taken into account in researches hitherto.

It may be that the extraversion–introversion dimension as described by Eysenck has little relevance to teaching success; perhaps it is concerned too much with social characteristics and insufficiently with cognitive ones. Various studies seem to suggest that extraverts are more attracted to teaching, but there are no clear indications that they do the job better than introverts. Warburton *et al.* (1963) suggest that, in selecting potential teachers, stability is more important than the extraversion–introversion dimension. It is to this that we turn in the next section.

Stability and teaching

Even at a superficial level there would seem to be a closer connection between this dimension and teaching success. The research indicates such a connection independent of the level at which the teaching is taking place. Happily all the evidence points in one direction.

Birkinshaw (1935) found that emotional stability was essential for a teacher to be successful. The classroom presents many frustrating and difficult situations in which the teacher has to maintain composure or in which great demands are made on patience. Barr (1945) found that 'personal emotional and social adjustment' was a major factor in predicting teaching efficiency, and other studies have shown that good adjustment on the part of the teacher helps to improve the adjustment of the pupils, and that, conversely, maladjustment in the teacher is associated either with absence of change or with change for the worse in the pupils.

Research with a variety of personality tests has confirmed this link. Soloman (1967), using the MPI, found that success in a teacher training course was positively linked with stability, and studies using the Guilford Personality Tests show that good teachers are more emotionally stable than ineffective ones, and indeed that teachers tend to be more emotionally stable than the non-teaching population!

The use of the 16 PF test enables us to consider source traits associated with stability. Cattell claimed that teachers as an occupational group were more good-natured and easy-going than average. He found them higher on source trait A, a largely hereditary trait making them more warm-hearted, expressive, co-operative and adaptable. Other studies have found significant correlations between being a good teacher and scoring highly on factor G (Barr *et al.*, 1961; Warburton *et al.*, 1963; Davis and Satterly, 1969). This factor includes a loading for emotional stability as well as for conscientiousness and sense of responsibility. Davis and Satterly found that Homerton students who gained low teaching grades were high in anxiety, making their behaviour tense, excitable and restless. Start (1966) found that the best teachers were above average in being relaxed and secure, and Lamke (1951) found that cheerfulness and emotional responsiveness were marks of the good teacher. It is of course difficult to say whether the feelings of security and cheerfulness were the causes of the good teaching or its effects. Being co-operative and friendly, both of which are signs of good adjustment, are frequently cited in studies of the good teacher.

On the MMPI, which contains a scale for measuring depressive tendencies, Schmid (1950) found a link between high depression scores and low ratings for teaching ability among female subjects. Using the same instrument, Moore and Cole (1957) concluded that poor practice-teaching performance was linked with a wide variety of maladjustments and emotional difficulties. These needed therapy

92

before successful teaching could be expected.

A major study of American teachers carried out by Ryans (1960) found that those teachers rated as 'good' had superior emotional adjustment to the rest of the large sample (N=6,000). Again there is a suspicion of circularity here in that teaching well and being adjusted to one's work seem necessarily to accompany each other. Overall, however, stability, whether brought about primarily through temperamental or environmental factors, is clearly related to success in teaching. The stable person, who, according to Eysenck, is likely to be controlled, reliable, even-tempered, calm, easy-going, carefree and a leader, seems best fitted to make a successful teacher.

The good teacher

We still have a far-from-complete picture of the good teacher, but there is more to be said. Although Eysenck's dimensions seem to provide a more useful framework for discussing successful pupils than successful teachers, there have been other attempts to find the pattern of personality that makes for success in teaching and much has been written of a speculative nature on the subject. The last decade has seen a growing disenchantment with experiment in psychology and a new recognition of the place of introspection and speculation (Joynson, 1972). Certainly at this stage in our thinking about the good teacher, empirical studies need to be complemented by the speculations of experienced educationists.

The extensive American Teacher Characteristics Study (Ryans, 1960) identified three groups of teachers rated high, low and average in teaching ability. The high ability teachers were distinguished from the rest in various ways: they were very generous in their appraisal of the behaviour and motives of other people rather than critical and nega-

93

tive in their attitudes towards them. Highet (1951) suggests that once a teacher stops liking his pupils he should change his job.

The Ryans study also showed that the good teachers had strong interests in the arts—they were cultured and enjoyed literature, music, painting, etc. They participated in social groups and enjoyed their relationships with their pupils. Their command of language was above average, suggesting a high level of articulateness and skill in verbal communication, and their classroom procedures were less authoritarian than average. Warburton's (Warburton *et al.*, 1963) conclusion that in selecting potential teachers it is best to concentrate on the applicants' general cultural level than on their level of ability and on their participation in social activities rather than on their social or domestic background bears out the American findings. As Highet (1951) puts it: 'The good teacher is an interesting man or woman.'

Other studies in America, using the Guilford-Martin Personality Inventories, have shown good teachers to be higher than average in such characteristics as friendliness and skill in personal relations, in objectivity, agreeableness and co-operativeness. Teachers as a whole seem to be higher in these traits than the population at large, and the best teachers higher than teachers in general. Reducing the findings to a crude statement—it seems that the good teacher is a pleasant man or woman.

He also seems to be a lively sort of person. His interests and his active social life will contribute to this and prevent his becoming jaded and dull. Researches have shown that personal pace is linked with success: Jones (1956), for example, found that good teachers seem to prefer a rapid pace and to like quickness of action and efficiency. Soloman (1967) refers to the 'live-wire' quality of the good teacher. Such a trait is surely essential if one is to succeed in stimulating others. It is contact with lively minds that produces the thinking individual.

Birkinshaw (1935) suggested yet another characteristic of the good teacher: it is important, she says, for the teacher to be able 'to stand aside placidly whilst others do badly what she can do well herself'. This suggests a certain patience and the ability to put oneself in another's place and so appreciate problems which for oneself have long since disappeared.

Those characteristics associated with maturity (see chapter 5) seem to have relevance for success in teaching. A variety of autonomous interests, the extension of the self, is supported by the research evidence, as is the capacity to view oneself objectively. Plainly having a sense of purpose and direction, a unifying philosophy of life, is also desirable, so long as it does not make the teacher intolerant of other sets of convictions. Indeed, the capacity to modify one's philosophy of life in the light of new ideas is something which any good teacher must safeguard. The closed mind makes good teaching, as well as learning, an impossibility.

8

Teacher–pupil interaction

The main purpose of this book has been to consider questions relating to effectiveness in learning and teaching. What makes for success as a pupil and what makes for success in teaching? We have tried to move towards an answer to these questions by considering personality, and various accounts have been given of it. We have looked at traits of personality which seem to be related to effectiveness. Our prime concern in this last chapter is to look at the relationship between learner and teacher. It is not enough to consider the personality of one or the other, though to do so is valuable. The next, and vital, step is to consider what happens when these two personalities meet and have to evolve a system of interaction. In every case the interaction will be different, and this makes the subject highly complex. The many relationships among widely differing pupil and teacher characteristics, plus the influences of the task undertaken and the school environment, make our quest for the successful pupil and the effective teacher seem like a wild-goose chase.

However, recent research into social interaction is providing help. It means that well-meaning and interesting discussions of the teacher–pupil relationship, such as that by Baxter (1950), and more empirically based studies, such as that by Bush (1954), are capable of being advanced still further in the light of findings in the social psychology of interacting persons. Some of Baxter's opinions, for example that a friendly classroom atmosphere is conducive to effective teaching and learning, have received empirical support, so that insight is now backed by observable evidence. This is a much more satisfactory state of affairs in the modern climate of opinion.

The last two decades have produced many findings which point to the value of the study of personality and of interpersonal behaviour for those who work with people. This includes teachers. Teaching involves the transmission of information, academic skills and understanding to others, and to some extent this can be done better by a teaching machine than by a human being. The machine programme breaks down the subject-matter so that it can be systematically assimilated and caters for individual differences by enabling each pupil to proceed at his own rate. But, as Borger and Seaborne (1966) remind us, any teacher who can effectively be replaced by a teaching machine deserves to be replaced. There is more to teaching than that. The teacher has the function of arousing motivation for learning, of awakening interests and of promoting creative thinking. He has also the important task of training people to live together harmoniously. How can he do this? His effectiveness depends on the interaction between him and his pupils.

It was suggested in the last chapter that a teacher must like his pupils. This seems like a truism. It comes as a surprise therefore to discover that some teachers who were exceedingly competent professionally were low in liking for their pupils. High liking for pupils is not essential for teaching competence (Bush, 1954). Indeed, high liking may be detrimental. If a teacher allows himself to become personally entangled with a pupil, or even a class, this may

97

destroy the objectivity which enables him to have insight into his pupils' problems. Having an interest in one's pupils is very different and is highly desirable. Bush found that those teachers who knew about such things as their pupils' health, aptitudes, aspirations, learning difficulties and background were more effective than those who had no such knowledge.

The case with pupils' liking for the teacher is different: this is positively correlated with success. If a pupil likes his teacher, it is probably that (1) he will like the subject taught (or, in the case of a general subject teacher, share his enthusiasms) and (2) he will make better progress. Pupils not only attain more under teachers they like, they *feel* they are learning more. In so far as learning by modelling or imitation plays any part in school learning, more of this will occur where the pupil likes the teacher, simply because we tend to identify with those we admire. Receptivity to ideas and information will also be greater in this situation.

Argyle (1967) claims that, because being liked is experienced as rewarding, A will like B if he sees that B likes him. This principle may be valid between two individuals, but in the classroom situation, Bush found no significant relationship between teacher's liking for pupil and pupil's liking for teacher. In the 650 cases he studied, a correlation of only $+0.27$ was found. Liking does not of itself breed liking: to be liked by his pupils, and therefore to improve their learning, a teacher must do much more than simply like them.

Popularity, like happiness, is a by-product: the teacher will not find it by direct seeking—it will come to him if he looks after other things. What are these things? How can a teacher get his pupils to like him?

In the ideal situation, it simply happens. Although there is a saying that opposites attract, this seems to apply only in respect of dominant and submissive persons where the one needs the other as a logical complement. In most cases, evidence shows that like attracts like: our friends are usually those with similar personality traits to our own. If people like others who are similar to themselves, it should be possible to match them. Bush found in the analysis of his data that a certain type of student tends to work successfully with one, rather than another, type of teacher.

Though it is at present impracticable, and likely to remain so, the matching of pupil and teacher is an interesting idea. On the basis of his evidence, Bush discerned three types of pupil. The first (Type A) is verbally able rather than practical; he plans to go to college; he seeks intellectual stimulation. His home is probably of a higher socioeconomic class than average. His emotional problems are few, his background stable and he mixes well with others. Much of this fits in with the standard conception of the typical English grammar school pupil. Ten to fifteen per cent of the 650 pupils in the three schools studied by Bush fitted this category. The type seems to be closely akin to Liam Hudson's 'converger' (Hudson, 1966). Convergers are more emotionally controlled and stable, and gain higher scores on standardized intelligence tests which have a verbal bias. They are more accurate and disciplined in their work habits.

The second type (Type B) tends to be not so well adjusted socially and is either apathetic or hostile towards schoolwork. Often he comes from a negative family situation where he has experienced rejection. His main need is for security and confidence, and until he has solved the crucial problems of his own circumstances he is unlikely to make progress in his academic work. As many as 20 to 25 per cent of pupils in Bush's study fell in this category.

The third type (Type C) may score highly in tests either

99

of verbal or of manipulative ability. He is definite and forthright in his opinions, even to the extent of being violent in his likes and dislikes. He is emotional, unconventional and tends to be unpopular with teachers. His main need seems to be to express his individuality in a creative or artistic way. Only five per cent of Bush's subjects were of this type. It seems to have affinities with Hudson's 'diverger' who is more impulsive, less emotionally controlled, more emphatic in statements of opinion, and less popular with his teachers.

Bush also found three types of teachers: Type A' who is subject-orientated, rather formal and of the 'let's-stick-to-the-business' type; Type B', primarily concerned with his pupils' social and emotional growth, subject-matter being secondary to this. He is more informal and friendly in his approach, more willing to work alongside his pupils than to remain aloof and ahead. Type C' wants to touch off the creative spark in his pupils. He tends to be artistic and emotional and to work by intuition.

To match pupil A with teacher A', B with B' and C with C' would seem a sound procedure. Joyce and Hudson (1968), working with medical students, found that in a majority of cases, convergers learned best from convergers and divergers from divergers. There are of course many other types, but this is a start. The difficulty lies in the impracticability of the project: with our present teacher–pupil ratio it simply could not be done. As often happens, the ideal must give way to a more realistic alternative. The teacher must be trained to meet the pupils' needs if blending of personalities does not occur spontaneously.

What makes interaction between two persons satisfying to both? The answer lies in the extent to which one is found rewarding by the other. Working under a particular teacher will be experienced as rewarding by the pupil if the teacher is able to meet his needs in some way.

Both cognitive needs (relating to knowing) and affective needs (relating to feeling) must be met, in differing proportions according to pupil-type (for example, Type A's needs are primarily cognitive, Type B's affective). In what do these needs consist, and how can the teacher prepare himself to meet them?

All pupils need to find in their teacher the fulfilment of their cognitive needs. For this the teacher must have the two attributes of *cognitive validity* and *motivating power*.

(1) By cognitive validity is meant appearing to know what one's role presupposes one should know. The teacher of physics should seem to his pupils to be knowledgeable about physics, and also about ways of organizing and presenting the subject-matter so as to make it 'digestible' by his pupils. The image of competence presented by the teacher is an important condition of teacher effectiveness.

(2) By motivating power is meant the ability to stimulate the pupils to want to learn. The good teacher will find ways of arousing interest, curiosity and intellectual excitement. He may do this by initial questioning and the presenting of problems to which most of his pupils would like to know the answer. In this way a slight sense of anxiety is produced. The pupil's psychological equilibrium is disturbed and is likely to remain so until a way of solving the problem is found. Knowing the kinds of things his pupils are naturally interested in will help the teacher to select appropriate questions to arouse motivation.

Pupils need to have their affective or emotional needs met by the teacher. As we have seen, liking for the teacher is a prerequisite of the most effective learning. What emotional needs must be met before liking can come about? There are two main ones: the *need for security* and the *need to find the relationship rewarding*.

(1) Security will be needed more by the less self-assured child, but every pupil needs to feel secure. If the teacher

is highly unstable, pupils will not feel secure and little progress is likely (see chapter 7). If the teacher is highly punitive and frowns and shouts a good deal, an insecure atmosphere is built up in the class. The teacher who is attempting to work out his own emotional problems through his teaching will generate insecurity, for example the sexually frustrated person who becomes emotionally entangled with his pupils. Low anxiety on the part of the teacher, and poise, make for a secure atmosphere. The highly anxious teacher, whose anxiety is of the kind which springs largely from an attempt to appear other than he knows himself to be, is most unlikely to meet his pupils' need for security. Ways in which this anxiety communicates itself to the pupils are discussed later in this chapter.

(2) The need to find the relationship rewarding can be met only if pupil and teacher use styles of behaviour which blend, mesh or synchronize. For example, if both parties wish to be dominant, a clash will occur; if one is dominant and the other submissive, meshing is likely: the two styles are complementary. If A wishes to talk a good deal and B prefers to listen, the styles will be mutually rewarding. For his relationship with his pupil to be effective, the teacher may need to change his usual style of interaction to the point where meshing occurs. The greater therefore his repertoire of social techniques, the more general his success.

Towards effective teacher–pupil interaction

To teach effectively the teacher must first establish rapport with his pupils. Sometimes rapport will be needed with the class as a whole, at other times with a group or with an individual. Rapport depends on a number of factors.

(1) First is what may be called *perceptual sensitivity*. This refers to the ability to perceive other persons

102

accurately; it has been shown to be linked with popularity. Women show more interest in the interpersonal aspects of behaviour, but there is no evidence that they have greater perceptual sensitivity than men. Both are equally capable of missing a great number of important cues. When two persons interact, attention is paid first and foremost to the speech component of the interaction. However, there are subtler components. We have for so long concentrated on the verbal content of interaction that we have become insensitive to the non-verbal elements which in other animals are primary cues in interaction. We have to learn the non-verbal code after first being made aware of its existence. Facial expressions, gestures, tone of voice and inflexion, all have important messages to convey. Perceptual sensitivity refers to our ability to interpret these. It is obviously important for the teacher; being able to interpret such non-verbal messages from his pupils should help him to adjust his technique accordingly. People can be given training in sensitivity. This has been done through the use of tapes. Davitz (1964) found that training could improve accuracy of identifying emotions from taped speeches having neutral content. This focused the subject's attention on the non-verbal elements of speech with no visual cues. Other investigators, Jecker et al. (1965), trained teachers to judge more accurately from film whether children understood what they were being taught. The subjects' attention was drawn to the facial expressions and gestures which usually indicate understanding, and thus their perceptual sensitivity was increased. T-groups are a well-established method of sensitivity training aimed at improving the participants' awareness of the emotional reactions of others in the group. Studies of T-groups show little evidence of increased accuracy in person perception, although improved interpersonal skills in the work situation have been noted. They may therefore be of value in improving teacher effectiveness, though it must be added that T-groups can generate an emotional dynamite which has produced nervous breakdowns in some participants.

(2) For rapport with many different individuals, the teacher needs *a wide repertoire of social techniques*. Having, through his perceptual sensitivity, received cues from his pupils, he must adjust his style of interaction to fit. The feedback must be used to produce corrective action. Thus cues indicating lack of understanding must lead the teacher to make the point slowly in another way. Cues indicating pupil resistance must call out persuasive techniques. Cues indicating that the pupil has a poor self-image must elicit encouragement and reassurance. A teacher who wants to have a friendly relationship with his pupil must change his style with a pupil who is low in affiliation and does not desire friendship. A dependent style must be met with support. The teacher must be 'all things to all men' for effective interaction to occur. The extent to which he can do this is probably dependent on his personality: he needs to be sufficiently flexible and ingenious to make such changes of style and technique smoothly and without too much personal cost.

(3) The teacher must engineer the *optimum emotional atmosphere*. The frequently quoted study by Lippitt and White (1958) showed how the democratic atmosphere, as opposed to the authoritarian or *laissez-faire* one, produced better morale and good work. Argyle (1967) points out that when dominance and high affiliation are combined in a person the resulting social behaviour is that of one who advises, co-ordinates, directs, leads and initiates. This would seem to be an ideal teaching strategy. Dominance without high affiliation results either in antagonism or withdrawal. It would seem therefore that the best technique for the teacher is a warm-dominant one. This will show itself

in firm and confident classroom behaviour with strong overtones of support and friendliness. The teacher must be positive; he must play a very active part in the relationship. At the same time, he must not make his pupils feel bombarded or overpowered. Energy and powers of initiation have been found to be important attributes of social competence and are surely valuable in teaching. The teacher must remember, however, that he may need to restrain himself in order to increase the involvement of his pupils. Research shows that to get others to talk, one needs to talk less oneself, to ask open-ended questions, i.e. those which invite longer answers, to mention subjects known to be of interest to the others and to reward anything said by approving gestures such as smiling, looking and nodding.

(4) Rapport is more likely where the teacher *operates smoothly and is in perfect control of social techniques.* This ability is likely to increase with practice. In some cases it may fail to develop at all, especially in highly anxious persons. Emotional arousal above a certain limit is known to interfere with effectiveness in motor skills and in problem-solving: it will also affect social interaction adversely. High anxiety communicates itself through movements, speech and voice. Eye-contact is low in highly anxious persons: the teacher will tend not to look at his pupils, thereby reducing his chances of involving them. His movements will be jerky and his bodily posture tense and awkward. Clumsiness will be increased. His speech will be fast, there will be a good deal of hesitation and his utterances will tend to be short, his tone breathy. The anxious person tends to talk more loudly and in a higher register. These emotional aspects of speech are likely to promote feelings of uncomfortableness in pupils and make contact with the anxious person unrewarding. Speech style is obviously important in promoting effec-

tive interaction. Joos (1962) suggested five styles of speech : the Intimate, the Casual-personal, the Social-consultative, the Formal and the Frozen. The more informal styles are effective in establishing relationships and maintaining these, whilst the formal styles are better for conveying information. Obviously a teacher will need to change his style according to his purpose and the feedback received. Flexibility and sensitivity would appear to be important in this respect.

Conclusion

We have seen that success in learning and in teaching depends greatly on the nature of teacher–pupil interaction. Sometimes harmonious interaction occurs naturally, as in friendship; at other times, modification of styles must take place to secure meshing. Pupils are less likely to modify their techniques than teachers (a) because they are usually less capable of doing so, and (b) because it is the teacher's task to arouse motivation. The crucial question is : how far can teachers be trained in effective interaction and how far is it a function of their temperament? That learning to interact effectively is possible is suggested by the fact that competence in social skills increases with the years; it is not static but affected by practice. However, certain personality types will find it easier to adopt a variety of interactional techniques and to identify the cues which make certain styles desirable. The latter depends on sensitivity and the former on resourcefulness and flexibility. These seem to the writer to be essential for good teacher–pupil relationships.

No teacher in Bush's study was effective with all the pupils in his class. Probably the truth is that no teacher *can* be successful with everyone, though some teachers may find this hard to accept. There cannot be one kind

106

of effective teacher because there are so many interactional variables. As with friendship, so with teaching: people are not so much liked for what they are intrinsically as for what they are able to do for each other when interacting. A teacher is not a good teacher simply because he has certain characteristics but because of an indefinable something that comes into play when teacher and taught interact.

Suggestions for further reading

I have limited these to four books. They are all closely linked with the theme of this book and are strongly recommended.

M. Argyle, *The Psychology of Interpersonal Behaviour*, Penguin, 1967.

A good introduction to the subtle non-verbal communication that comes into play when people interact. This area of psychology has important implications for teachers, concerned as they are with social skills. The extent to which they can master these skills will contribute to their success in their daily work. There is a brief section on teaching as a social skill.

C. S. Hall and G. Lindzey, *Theories of Personality*, 2nd edn, Wiley: N.Y., 1970.

An admirable book serving as a fairly detailed introduction to the broad field of personality. After an opening chapter on the nature of personality theory, the authors deal with the structure, dynamics and development of personality as proposed by various psychologists. Each chapter ends with a look at the current status of the particular theory and a brief evaluation. The final chapter tries to identify the general trends existing despite wide differences among individual theories and speculates briefly on the future development of personality theory in view of the missing qualities in the present field. The book is comprehensive, well-written and interesting to read.

G. Highet, *The Art of Teaching*, Methuen, 1951.

This is a book which, as its title suggests, shows the limitations of any attempt to make a scientific analysis of teaching. Teaching involves values which are outside the grasp of science: psychologists need to heed this. The sections on the qualities of the good teacher and on methods of communication are particularly valuable for the student-teacher.

A. Storr, *The Integrity of the Personality*, Heinemann, 1960 (Penguin, 1963).

An excellent book particularly for the way it deals with the mature relationship. If teaching is, as I believe, essentially a matter of relationships, then the nature of these is crucial. Anthony Storr sets before us an ideal type of relationship, essentially one for adults but one which, none the less, has implications at all educational levels. Recognizing and respecting differences from oneself is central to good relationships. It pre-supposes self-knowledge which needs to begin in early childhood. Becoming one's real self and developing a mature dependence on others are key processes in living fully. All teachers are concerned with both: all should read this important book.

Bibliography

ADLER, A. (1929), *Problems of Neurosis*, Kegan Paul.

ADLER, A. (1932), *What Life Should Mean to You*, Unwin.

ADLER, A. (1939), *Social Interest*, Putnam, N.Y.

ALLPORT, G. W. (1937), *Personality: a psychological interpretation*, Holt, N.Y.

ALLPORT, G. W. (1963), *Pattern and Growth in Personality*, Holt International, N.Y.

ALLPORT, G. W. (1971), in 'Gordon Allport—a conversation' by R. I. Evans, *Psychology Today*, 4, Del Mar, California.

ALTUS, W. D. (1966), 'Birth order and its sequelae', *Science*, 151.

ANSBACHER, H. L. and R. (eds) (1956), *The Individual Psychology of Alfred Adler*, Basic Books, N.Y.

ARGYLE, M. (1967), *The Psychology of Interpersonal Behaviour*, Penguin.

ASTINGTON, E. (1960), 'Personality assessments and academic performance in a boys' grammar school', *British Journal of Educational Psychology*, 30.

BARKER, R. G., DEMBO, T. and LEWIN, K. (1941), 'Frustration and regression: an experiment with young children', *Univ. Iowa Studies in Child Welfare*, 18.

BARR, A. S. (1945), 'The measurement of teaching ability', *Journal of Experimental Education*, 14.

BARR, A. S. *et al.* (1961), 'Wisconsin studies of the measurement and prediction of teacher effectiveness', *Journal of Experimental Education*, 30.

BAXTER, B. (1950), *Teacher–Pupil Relationships*, Macmillan, N.Y.

BIRKINSHAW, M. (1935), *The Successful Teacher*, Hogarth Press.

BORGER, R. and SEABORNE, A. E. M. (1966), *The Psychology of Learning*, Penguin.

BROWN, J. A. C. (1961), *Freud and the Post-Freudians*, Penguin.

BUSH, R. N. (1954), *The Teacher–Pupil Relationship*, Prentice-Hall, N.Y.

CATTELL, J. M. and BRIMHALL, D. R. (1921), *American Men of Science*, Science Press, N.Y.

CATTELL, R. B. (1965), *The Scientific Analysis of Personality*, Penguin.

CATTELL, R. B. *et al.* (1966), 'What can personality and motivation source trait measurements add to the prediction of school achievement?', *British Journal of Educational Psychology*, 36.

CENTRAL ADVISORY COUNCIL FOR EDUCATION (1967), *Children and Their Primary Schools* (Plowden Report), HMSO.

CHILD, D. (1964), 'The relationship between introversion and extra-version, neuroticism and performance in school examinations', *British Journal of Educational Psychology*, 34.

COGHILL, N. (trs.) (1951), *The Canterbury Tales*, Penguin.

CORTIS, G. A. (1968), 'Predicting student performance in Colleges of Education', *British Journal of Educational Psychology*, 38.

CROCKER, A. C. (1968), 'Predicting teacher success', *Education for Teaching*, 76.

DAVIS, T. and SATTERLY, D. J. (1969), 'Personality profiles of student teachers', *British Journal of Educational Psychology*, 39.

DAVITZ, J. R. (1964), *The Communication of Emotional Meaning*, McGraw-Hill, N.Y.

DEPARTMENT OF EDUCATION AND SCIENCE (1972), *Teacher Education and Training* (James Report), HMSO.

ENTWISTLE, N. J. and CUNNINGHAM, S. (1968), 'Neuroticism and school attainment—a linear relationship?', *British Journal of Educational Psychology*, 38.

ENTWISTLE, N. J. and D. (1970), 'The relationships between personality, study methods and academic performance', *British Journal of Educational Psychology*, 40.

ENTWISTLE, N. J. and WELSH, J. (1969), 'Correlates of school attainment at different ability levels', *British Journal of Educational Psychology*, 39.

ENTWISTLE, N. J. and WILSON, J. D. (1970), 'Personality, study methods and academic performance', *Universities Quarterly*, 24.

ERIKSON, E. H. (1959), 'Identity and the life cycle', *Psychological Issues*, 1.

ERIKSON, E. H. (1963), *Childhood and Society*, 2nd edn, Norton, N.Y.

EYSENCK, H. J. (1953), *Uses and Abuses of Psychology*, Penguin.

EYSENCK, H. J. (1957), *Sense and Nonsense in Psychology*, Penguin.

EYSENCK, H. J. (1959), 'Personality and problem solving', *Psychological Reports*, 5; also in *Readings in Extraversion–Introversion*, vol. 2 : *Fields of Application*, Staples, 1971.

EYSENCK, H. J. (1960), *The Structure of Human Personality*, 2nd edn, Methuen.

EYSENCK, H. J. (1964), *Crime and Personality*, Routledge & Kegan Paul.

EYSENCK, H. J. and RACHMAN, S. (1965a), *Causes and Cures of Neurosis*, Routledge & Kegan Paul.

EYSENCK, H. J. (1965b), *Fact and Fiction in Psychology*, Penguin.

EYSENCK, H. J. and COOKSON, D. (1969), 'Personality in primary school children', *British Journal of Educational Psychology*, 39.

EYSENCK, H. J. and S. G. B. (1969), *Personality Structure and Measurement*, Routledge & Kegan Paul.

FARLEY, F. H. (1966), 'Individual differences in solution time in error-free problem solving', *British Journal of Social and Clinical Psychology*, 5.

FARRELL, B. A. (1970), 'Psychoanalytic theory', in S. G. M. Lee and M. Herbert (eds), *Freud and Psychology*, Penguin.

FREUD, S. (1924), *A General Introduction to Psychoanalysis*, Boni & Liveright (reprinted 1953, Permabooks, N.Y.).

FURNEAUX, W. D. (1962), 'The psychologist and the university', *Universities Quarterly*, 17.

GETZELS, J. W. and JACKSON, P. W. (1963), 'The teacher's personality and characteristics', in N. L. Gage (ed.), *Handbook of Research on Teaching*, Rand McNally, Chicago.

GLUECK, S. and E. T. (1959), *Predicting Delinquency and Crime*, Harvard University Press (1960, Oxford).

GORER, G. (1966), 'Psychoanalysis in the world', in C. Rycroft (ed.), *Psychoanalysis Observed*, Constable (1968, Penguin).

GUNTRIP, H. (1971), *Psychoanalytic Theory, Therapy and the Self*, Hogarth Press.

HALL, C. S. and LINDZEY, G. (1957), *Theories of Personality*, Wiley, N.Y.

HARTMANN, H. (1958), *Ego Psychology and the Problem of Adaptation*, International Universities Press, N.Y.

HEBB, D. O. (1949), *The Organization of Behaviour*, Wiley, N.Y.

HEBB, D. O. (1951), 'The role of neurological ideas in psychology', *Journal of Personality*, 20.

HIGHET, G. (1951), *The Art of Teaching*, Methuen.

HOLT, R. R. (1962), 'Individuality and generalization in the psychology of personality', *Journal of Personality*, 30; also in R. S. Lazarus and E. M. Opton (eds), *Personality*, Penguin, 1967.

HOOKER, H. F. (1931), 'A study of the only child at school', *Journal of Genetic Psychology*, 39.

HORE, T. (1971), 'Assessment of teaching practice: an "attractive" hypothesis', British Journal of Educational Psychology, 41.

HUDSON, L. (1966), Contrary Imaginations: a psychological study of the English schoolboy, Methuen (1968, Penguin).

HUDSON, L. (1968), Frames of Mind: ability, perception and self-perception in the arts and sciences, Methuen (1970, Penguin).

INKELES, A. (1963), 'Sociology and psychology', in S. Koch (ed.), Psychology: a study of a science, McGraw-Hill, N.Y.

James Report, see DEPARTMENT OF EDUCATION AND SCIENCE.

JECKER, J. D. et al. (1965), 'Improving accuracy in interpreting non-verbal cues of comprehension', Psychology in the Schools, 2.

JONES, E. (1953), The Life and Work of Sigmund Freud, Hogarth Press.

JONES, M. L. (1956), 'Analysis of certain aspects of teaching ability', Journal of Experimental Education, 25.

JOOS, M. (1962), 'The five clocks', International Journal of American Linguistics, 28, part V.

JOYCE, C. R. B. and HUDSON, L. (1968), 'Student style and teacher style', British Journal of Medical Education, 2.

JOYNSON, R. B. (1972), 'The return of mind', Bulletin of the British Psychological Society, 25.

JUNG, C. G. (1923), Psychological Types, Kegan Paul.

KLINE, P. (1966), 'Extraversion, neuroticism and academic perform-ance among Ghanaian university students', British Journal of Educational Psychology, 36.

KLINE, P. and GALE, A. (1971), 'Extraversion, neuroticism and per-formance in a psychology examination', British Journal of Educa-tional Psychology, 41.

LAING, R. D. (1960), The Divided Self, Tavistock (1968, Penguin).

LAMKE, T. A. (1951), 'Personality and teaching success', Journal of Experimental Education, 20.

LIPPITT, R. and WHITE, R. K. (1958), 'An experimental study of leadership and group life', in E. E. Maccoby, T. M. Newcomb and E. L. Hartley (eds), Readings in Social Psychology, Holt, N.Y.

LYNN, R. and GORDON, I. E. (1961), 'The relation of neuroticism and extraversion to intelligence and educational attainment', British Journal of Educational Psychology, 31.

MCKELLAR, P. (1968), Experience and Behaviour, Penguin.

MACMURRAY, J. (1935), Reason and Emotion, Faber.

MOORE, C. J. and COLE, D. (1957), 'The relation of M.M.P.I. scores to practice teacher ratings', Journal of Educational Research, 50.

BIBLIOGRAPHY

MORRIS, B. S. (ed.) (1956), 'Freud, Jung and Adler: their relevance to the teacher's life and work', *New Era*, 37.

MORRIS, B. S. (1966), 'The contribution of psychology to education', in J. W. Tibble (ed.), *The Study of Education*, Routledge & Kegan Paul.

MORRIS, B. S. (1972), 'Personality study for students of education', chapter 8 in *Objectives and Perspectives in Education*, Routledge & Kegan Paul.

NOTCUTT, B. (1953), *The Psychology of Personality*, Methuen.

Plowden Report, see CENTRAL ADVISORY COUNCIL FOR EDUCATION.

RIDDING, L. W. (1967), 'An investigation of personality measures associated with over- and under-achievement in English and Arithmetic', *British Journal of Educational Psychology*, 37.

RUSHTON, J. (1966), 'The relationship between personality characteristics and scholastic success in eleven-year-old children', *British Journal of Educational Psychology*, 36.

RYANS, D. G. (1960), *Characteristics of Teachers*, American Council on Education, Washington, D.C.

SAVAGE, R. D. (1966), 'Personality factors and academic attainment in junior school children', *British Journal of Educational Psychology*, 36.

SCHACHTER, S. (1959), *The Psychology of Affiliation*, Stanford U.P.

SCHAFER, R. *et al.* (1951), 'Report on a survey of current psychological test practices', supplement to *Newsletter*, Division of Clinical and Abnormal Psychology, American Psychological Association, 4.

SCHMID, J. (1950), 'Factor analysis of prospective teachers' differences', *Journal of Experimental Education*, 18.

SEARS, R. R. (1944), 'Experimental analyses of psychoanalytic phenomena', in J. McV. Hunt (ed.), *Personality and the Behaviour Disorders*, Ronald Press, N.Y.

SINGER, A. (1954), 'Social competence and success in teaching', *Journal of Experimental Education*, 23.

SINGH, A. H. (1969), 'Interests, values and personality traits of students specializing in different fields of study in university', *British Journal of Educational Psychology*, 39.

SKINNER, B. F. (1971), *Beyond Freedom and Dignity*, Knopf, N.Y. (1972, Cape).

SOLOMAN, E. (1965), 'Personality factors and attitudes of mature training college students', M.Ed. thesis, Manchester University.

SOLOMAN, E. (1967), research note, *British Journal of Educational Psychology*, 37.

SPIEL, O. (1962), *Discipline without Punishment*, Faber.

114

STAFFORD-CLARK, D. (1967), *What Freud Really Said*, Penguin.

START, K. B. (1966), 'The relation of teaching ability to measures of personality', *British Journal of Educational Psychology*, 36.

STORR, A. (1960), *The Integrity of the Personality*, Heinemann (1963, Penguin).

STORR, A. (1966), 'The concept of cure', in C. Rycroft (ed.), *Psychoanalysis Observed*, Constable (1968, Penguin).

TAYLOR, P. H. (1962), 'Children's evaluations of the characteristics of the good teacher', *British Journal of Educational Psychology*, 32.

THIGPEN, C. H. and CLECKLEY, H. (1957), *Three Faces of Eve*, McGraw-Hill, N.Y.

THOMAN, W. (1970), 'Birth order rules all', *Psychology Today*, 4, Del Mar, California.

TROWN, E. A. (1970), 'Some evidence on the interaction between teaching strategy and personality', *British Journal of Educational Psychology*, 40.

VAIHINGER, H. (1925), *The Philosophy of 'As If'*, Harcourt, Brace & World, N.Y.

VERNON, J. (1965), *Inside the Black Room: studies of sensory deprivation*, Souvenir Press (1966, Penguin).

WARBURTON, F. W., BUTCHER, H. J. and FORREST, G. M. (1963), 'Predicting student performance in a university department of education', *British Journal of Educational Psychology*, 33.